DEDICATION

This book is dedicated to my beloved grandfather, John J. McStravick, and my sister, Betsy. I cannot imagine what my life would have been without them. I love them so very much and miss them with all my heart.

FOREWORD

Years ago, I met Mary when she began coming to our church either for Sunday service or our midweek Eucharist. The thing that was so unusual about her attendance was that she could not enter the nave of the church during the celebration of the Eucharist—or Holy Communion. We had a narthex or lobby area that opened into the nave. Mary could sit there, but she could not enter the church without feeling physically ill. It was obvious that this kind of manifestation in the sacramental presence of Jesus was nothing short of demonic oppression.

I am not an exorcist, and I do not consider this to be an area of gifting in my ministry, but I am also not one to shy away from a spiritual battle when confronted by the forces of evil. I do know enough to know that nothing will effectively happen in deliverance or exorcism unless or until the person is ready to proceed, so I never force the issue. I waited for Mary for quite some time. She would just come to church and sit in the lobby.

On one Wednesday morning, Mary asked me to hear her confession before noon Eucharist. I would hear her confession at the altar rail, and she would leave for the lobby before we actually started the midweek service. As we began what I expected to be a brief sacramental confession, all hell suddenly broke loose. I asked Mary if she was ready, and she responded immediately that she was—she never asked, "Ready for what?" We both knew in our spirits that it was time for her deliverance.

I may not have been ready for what followed, but the Holy Spirit was. The only people to come into that service that day were all seasoned, spiritually mature, praying Christians. And then, a psychologist who was a member of our parish but lived a far distance away—and never came to midweek service—suddenly came in to assist me; I knew God was orchestrating what was happening.

Up to that point in my ministry, I had not encountered anything as dramatic as I did with Mary's exorcism. Her facial contortions, the voices, and the begging, pleading, and lying of the spirits were not like anything that I had ever experienced. But the grace of the Holy Spirit was so heavy upon Mary that there was no fear or hesitation. Mary's face contorted into another person, and a man's voice came out of her mouth. I was able to address Mary at some times and the male voice at others. At one point, Mary talked about a bear; she saw approaching her, and she described it. The psychologist and I looked at each other, but we had no idea what Mary was talking about.

As the male voice became dominant, it began naming various minor demons at my command. As these were expelled, I knew in my spirit that these were concealing a larger, more serious spirit. To my surprise, I found myself laughing at these pathetic spirits, which tended to infuriate them. Finally, I encountered what some exorcists would call the "prince." When I did, I knew immediately that we had finally come to the chief antagonist—it identified itself as "The Spirit of Death." It did not leave without attacking one of our church members in a way that I can only describe as a temper tantrum.

After the exorcism was over and Mary sat through the noon Eucharist, it was as if that thing was lurking just above the rafters. One of our members knelt for Communion when suddenly, she was forcefully pushed forward into the altar rail with a force I would describe as a mule kick. She didn't swoon or faint; she was forcibly pushed by an invisible force. She fell to the floor and turned the greenish color of death. As we prayed over her, her color returned, and we commanded that thing out of the building.

Immediately, after the exorcism ended, Mary's face and voice returned to normal. She looked radiant and calm, but to my surprise, she had absolutely no recollection of anything that had just transpired. I never mentioned the bear since I didn't understand it myself. But decades later, when I reconnected with Mary over coffee, I mentioned the bear. She was shocked because it had actually been a significant part of her childhood oppression and spiritual trauma.

That was a dramatic exorcism without a doubt, but this is not a story about the devil or demons—this is the story of God's grace and redemption. Mary's story is heart-wrenching; her life was more difficult than most of us can imagine, but the Bible says that where sin abounds, grace much more abounds.

Mary's story of God's love and grace and redemption should inspire every one of us. No matter what your life story involves, no matter what sins you have committed; Mary's story teaches us that no one is beyond the loving embrace of Jesus. I hope that God will use this book to touch your heart and soul.

Rev. Dr. Martin Eppard
Good Shepherd Anglican Church, Catonsville, MD

CHAPTER ONE

The Beginning

Train up a child in the way he should go, and
when he is old, he will not depart from it.

—Proverbs 22:6

My parents separated in 1957. I was about four years old, and my sister was three. I will always remember that day, even down to what I was wearing. I was so young but was so brokenhearted. I loved my parents so much, and I knew that I would hardly ever see my father anymore. He was a US Marine, and we were stationed in Quantico, Virginia. My father drove us to Maryland to live with my grandfather on my mother's side. Sadly, my maternal grandmother had died when my mother was about twelve, so my grandfather lived alone. My sister and I called him "Granny." I don't know how he got that nickname, but I think it was because one of my cousins couldn't say "granddad." He was a devout Roman Catholic, who came from County Antrim, Ireland. He had a lovely Irish brogue, but I didn't really know that until I was in my teens. My little friends who were allowed to visit me would sometimes say, "Your grandfather talks funny," but I didn't know what they were talking about. I actually wanted to hit them because I was so hurt that they were making fun of him. He had immigrated to the United States in 1917, so that he wouldn't have to fight for the British during World War I.

He had experienced so much persecution in Ireland because of his Catholicism, and sometimes, I would cry when he told us about it. He said he had to hide behind bushes and sneak to church because the British soldiers would pelt him with stones, and he was just a young child. That hurt me so much! My sister, Betsy, and I were just so "crazy" about him. He did everything for us, and my sister and I would have been lost without him. My grandfather gave me so much, but the greatest gift of all was my gift of faith!

I was totally devoted to my sister as well. We were very close. She was so adorable. Her little blonde bangs and her adorable dimples. I felt like I had to protect her. I wanted to, but I was only a year older. Our childhood was very difficult, but my sister, Betsy, my "Granny," and I were like "three peas in a pod." We went through a lot together as you will see. He always called the girls in the family "daugthas." I believe that was Gaelic for "daughters" if I am not mistaken. Granny could speak Gaelic when he first arrived in the United States but eventually lost it. Betsy and I would love to hear the few phrases he did remember. Granny only had a third-grade education, but he was very smart. He worked for the Baltimore Gas and Electric Company, and he was so well-liked by everyone there. I think he was a great success! Many of the men from his work would just come to the house to visit, and if anything needed to be done, they would do it. I remember that like yesterday. One of Granny's bosses stopped by to visit with him one Sunday afternoon. We were so happy to see him. Betsy and I told him he wasn't allowed to leave, so we hid his hat! I can't believe we did that. They teased Granny at work about that for quite a while. Granny retired in 1959. I was six years old, but I remember it like yesterday. He was terribly sad when he came home from his retirement party. The men gave him a gold-plated boiler cap and a beautiful watch. He was telling Betsy and me about the party, and he broke down and "cried," so we all did. It was very sad. Granny reminded me so much of the Irish actor from the 1930s and '40s named Barry Fitzgerald. Granny had the same mannerisms and the same brogue. I just never thought he "talked funny." I remember he would always say, "You have to go to church on "Sunda." I would love to hear him say that, and when he was very excited about something, Granny would rub his hand together just as Mr. Fitzgerald did in the 1944 movie "Going My Way." I can hardly watch that movie because it makes me cry. I miss my grandfather so badly and always will until the end of my days.

Uncle Jimmy was my mother's brother, and Aunt Jane was her older sister. Aunt Jane and Uncle Gene were married in 1952 and had three children when Betsy and I went to live with Granny. I just loved my cousins. Ellen was about my age, Tim was the middle child, and Kevin was the youngest. They would come to visit us, and we had a "ball." Of course, we always got in trouble because we found mischievous things to do like stealing apples off our neighbor's tree or my cousin Tim stealing some rocks out of one of the neighbor's driveway. The neighbor actually called my Granny and said, "I will call the police if he does that again!" Oh my gosh, can you imagine that? Most of the time, we just wouldn't go to bed when we were told to because it was such a "blast" just to be together. It was wonderful when they came to visit because it was so lonely most of the time for Betsy and me. Dad hardly ever came to see us, and Mom was out "partying most of the time." I know it was very hard to be divorced in the 1950s, but I really think she was looking for someone to love her and to marry her. She was very pretty and petite. She seemed to attract a lot of boyfriends, and Betsy and I would try to do bad things to get rid of them. We wanted our mother and father to get back together again. If her boyfriends ever tried to hit us, we would scream at them and tell them, "My father will kill you. Don't you dare hit us. We will tell him. He's a Marine!" I think they knew we meant it, and they would stop. On my father's very rare visits, he always asked me if any men had been around, and I told him, "Yes!" I didn't realize at the time that I should never have said that at all. I just didn't know how bad it was going to get.

My Uncle Jimmy had been a Marine too. He was very proud of the Marine Corps. It was his life-long ambition. Sadly, he had been given a dishonorable discharge because he was gay. He was discharged in 1951. It haunted him all of his life—just heartbreaking! In 1952, he had met my Uncle Lou, who was to be his partner for forty-five years. Betsy and I just loved Uncle Lou too. He was a very handsome man, as was my Uncle Jimmy, and was extremely funny. He would tell the most hilarious stories. I learned about homosexuality when I was seven years old because I had accidentally "walked in on them" when my mother and I went downtown to visit one day unannounced. I didn't say a word, just backed out of the apartment, and never let on that I knew anything. I didn't want to hurt or embarrass them at all. I did begin to understand why Uncle Jimmy was not allowed to be a Marine. I loved Uncle Jimmy and Uncle Lou so much. I was close to them all of my life. I was sorry for all of the discrimination and hurt that they went through. Even though I was a child, I understood that they suffered so much rejection as did my Betsy and I. Uncle Jimmy's nickname for me was "Mert." I just loved that. When I became an adult, Uncle Jimmy and I would talk about his guilt due to his gay lifestyle. One day, he asked me, "Mert, is my sin worse than yours?" I was surprised that he asked me. I thought it over and said, "Uncle Jimmy, our sin is exactly the same. I am not very Christian, but I do understand that. You sleep with a man, and I sleep with a man out of marriage. Both sins are the same." I told him that I had the same guilt he did because I knew I wasn't doing what our Lord and the church expected of me. I said, "But Uncle Jimmy, someday, we will figure it out," and I gave him a big hug and said, "Unc, let's go have a drink." And we did!

Uncle Lou always told the most amazing stories about his stint in the US Army. He was stationed in Korea during the war and was a switchboard operator. He said the bombs were falling and the noise was so bad and he was just pulling the switches out of the board as fast as he could. They were all trying to get the "hell out of there!" and he thought that was "it," but they all got out okay. It was "touch and go" as the North Koreans were right on their "tail." After that incident, he went to the army chaplain and tried to tell him that he was gay and that he needed to be discharged. The army chaplain said, "Forget it. You are not gay. We don't believe you." Uncle Lou said he was shocked that they wouldn't believe him. He kept trying to convince them, but to no avail, so he just had to stay in until the war ended. Thank God, he came home in one piece! Another interesting story about him was that he had been an actor in New York. I found that so fascinating. He landed the part of a German informant in the stage version of "Stalag 17." This play was about a German prison camp that was set during World War II, and Uncle Lou played the part of a planted German informant. Uncle Lou's character was shot in the end, and my Uncle Jimmy said he couldn't stop crying when he saw Uncle Lou lying there "dead." It was such a touching story. I will never forget it. I was so proud of Uncle Lou, and I always told him, "Uncle Lou, you should have stayed in the theater!" I think he would have had great success. I don't know why he left the stage really.

My father's parents were wonderful to Betsy and me, as well. We called them Grandmaw and Grandpaw. Sadly, they were very poor and had adopted seven children and had two biological children of their own. My father's biological mother was Grandmaw's sister, Blanch. She was not married, and the stigma of illegitimacy was terrible in that time period, so my grandmother adopted my father. Aunt Blanch, as I called her, was very nice too. My dad and mom did take us to visit her. My mother thought the world of her. She worked in a bar in Baltimore, and the owner's name was Mr. Benny. I remember he always smoked a huge cigar, and he was so nice. Betsy and I were allowed to sit at the end of the bar and have coke and potato chips. It was so fun! They were wonderful to us when we visited them. Grandmaw's and Grandpaw's two biological children were my Uncle PeeWee and my Aunt Julie. Dad's older siblings were usually away when we were there. They were much older and had their own lives by then. My uncle Mike was in the Marine Corps. He did tell me that he wanted to be "just like my father!" I loved them all so much. My mother did take us to see them quite often because I think she had a good time when she visited them, and I realize now that she wasn't scared there, and neither was I. Grandmaw used to make me fifteen pancakes. I loved her pancakes so much! I loved her so much, and I loved Grandpaw too. He had been a Virginia state trooper, but he came down with emphysema and had to stop working. He had such a terrible cough. As I said, my grandparents were very poor, and they didn't have indoor plumbing, so we always had to use the outhouse. This is like a Johnny-on-the-spot." The scary thing about it was that we were all afraid that snakes might inhabit it, especially when it was during the night and there was no light. I will never forget my grandparents nor my aunts and uncles too. My dad didn't often come to see us when we were visiting there. I do remember seeing him just a couple of times while visiting. If he did come, he was on leave, and we had such a good time. My dad had a car, and he would take us for long rides. We were so excited. I remember he took us to Glen Echo Amusement Park, which was about an hour away, and it was such a ball. Julie and PeeWee just loved it too. I will never forget seeing Dad and PeeWee on the bumper cars. I was so excited! Most of the time, something went wrong though. As I remember, it was Dad usually having an attack. It was so terribly sad. Grandpaw didn't have a lot of compassion about my Dad's attacks. I remember him saying to my dad, "You just feel guilty for not taking good care of your children. That is why you are shaking." I wish my Grandpaw understood what my Dad was going through, especially now looking back. I know my Dad may have felt guilt for not being there for me and Betsy, but he was terribly sick. Grandmaw and Grandpaw were very upset that I didn't have caring parents for sure. My little Aunt Julie, who was only about six years older than I, always got stuck watching us because mom or dad, or both, would just take off. We tried to be good for her because we felt bad that she had to watch us. I really loved her, and she and I would practice the jitterbug. Betsy and I got to be very good at it because of Julie. It was really cute, but my aunt Julie didn't get to have a childhood either. She was very grown-up by the time she was ten.

I also had a best friend, who lived up the street from us. Her name was Theresa, and she was very dear to me and Betsy, and so was her family. Theresa was more like a sister than a best friend. She was a year older than I, so she was a grade ahead of me in school. Theresa's father was a "hoot," and I just loved him. He made me laugh so much. He had such a dry sense of humor. Her mother was lovely and made me feel like I was really part of the family. They had a large family, and I loved them all. I was very fortunate that her mom and dad didn't keep Theresa from being our friend. I will never forget that. I can't tell you how many times I was told to leave someone's porch or not to come back to their house because I was "divorced" and not allowed to play with their children, or as one person said to me, "You are NOT wanted here! Don't come back!" I was just so used to it; I didn't even cry. I just left.

Granny sent us to a Catholic school, which was very lonely for me. Being a child of divorce in the 1950s was scandalous as I said, and most of the kids were not allowed to play with us. Their parents made sure of that. I did make one really good friend in my first-grade class, though. Her name was Dana, and she was so kind to me. I just loved her too, as I loved my friend Theresa. Sadly, one morning, I was in class, and Dana wasn't there. Sister Anne Marie told us that Dana had died the night before and that I was the only one who would be allowed to attend the funeral out of our school. I was so devastated. I didn't even know she was sick. She had leukemia. I will never forget her. On the first day of class, Dana took me by the hand and said, "I want you to sit by me." I was so proud because I was so used to being "snubbed" by most of the kids. Dana was a popular child, so I was amazed that she just ignored all the gossip and the hatred and wanted me for a best friend. I attended the funeral alone. I had no adult with me, and Dana's family was very upset to see that, so they took me under their wing and had me sit in the front row of the church with them. That was incredibly kind and understanding of them! The priest gave a very touching eulogy. He said that Dana was dearly loved and that she was with Jesus. I had decided on that day that I really didn't want to live anymore because I didn't really feel loved at all, but would be loved in heaven. I mean that sincerely. I just could hardly go on, and you will see why as the book unfolds.

One day, I met a little girl down the street while I was walking home alone from the movie theater. I will never forget her either. She and her family were Jewish. They invited me into their home and let me stay for tea and cookies. It touched me so deeply. She would play the violin for me, and I was just so impressed. Eventually, they learned that I was "divorced," and it didn't matter to them a bit. I was actually invited one Saturday to go to Temple with them. I was so amazed by that! The rabbi brought a "vessel" around for people to touch, but I would not. I felt for sure that God was inside of it, and

I didn't think I was worthy to do that. They had a large family, and her dad was wonderful to me. I remember that he only had one arm. I don't remember why. He invited me to come to dinner with them after the service. I think they had ten children if I am remembering correctly. It was just wonderful! I felt so accepted and wanted. God bless them so much! It was so wonderful to be accepted, and I will never forget their kindness to me!

I also made a really good friend in fourth grade named Kathy. She was so nice to me too. It was wonderful of her as she always invited me to dinner. I was always hungry because most of the time my mother wasn't around so Betsy and I would wait for Granny to come home with groceries. He always had a paper bag full of groceries, and Betsy and I would run down the street and get the grocery bag from him because we knew he had to be tired, and we didn't want him to carry it up the street. We were so little, but we struggled and got that bag home no matter what it took. After all, he was in his late sixties or early seventies at that time and was a caddie at a golf course across town. He wouldn't get home sometimes until eight or nine o'clock at night, and he would make dinner for us. He could make a good Irish stew and also potato salad. I don't know how he did that. Work was his life. I think he was very sad and had been about forty-six when my grandmother died. He raised his three children alone, and now, he was stuck with raising Betsy and me. My parents more or less dumped the whole responsibility on him. I know he didn't want that, and I was so often the target of his burden. He loved me, but I know he resented me. If only I hadn't been born. My mother always called me a "Tommie Graves bastard" when she got upset or something bad was happening. I know she hated being married to my father and hated me too, I think. I knew what a "bastard" was because I ask a boy up the street. I couldn't hardly carry that on my little shoulders. I was so little, but I knew what my parents were doing was really wrong. I don't think either of them wanted the responsibility of children, and they were "dumping" it all on my Granny.

I really loved my little friends as I was very lonely as a child, as I mentioned earlier. My parents were hardly ever around, so my sister, Granny, and my friends meant everything to me. Uncle Jimmy and Uncle Lou did too. They would almost always come on Sunday to take us out somewhere. I think they really felt bad for us that we were alone so much. Theresa and I were together a lot. Sometimes, Theresa would say to me, "Do you want to go somewhere and just be sad with me?" I didn't know Theresa was sad as a child too. I'm very sorry that she was. We had such a deep connection and understanding of each other even as young as we were. We were very devout children and loved to go to church and talk about the saints. I just cannot imagine how lonely I would have been without Theresa and, of course, my Betsy and my Granny too.

I hated my school, but two of the nuns were really wonderful to me, and I had two lay teachers who really cared for me. I am very grateful for my excellent Catholic school education. Most of all, I am so grateful for the gift of faith that I received through my grandfather, my aunt, and the Church. I loved Jesus so much and the Blessed Mother! I loved to read about the lives of the saints. Granny would pray with us every night and bless the rooms with holy water. He truly lived his faith. He went to Mass every morning before going to work. My grandfather never learned how to drive, so he always depended on the buses. In the early 1950s, before I was born, Granny was sitting in the front of the bus, and an African American lady got on the bus, but there were no seats. He told us that he gave her his seat, and the bus driver physically threw him off the bus. He had such pity for the woman and was so intolerant of the racism. He taught us to love all people. He was also appalled at the extreme dislike of a Jewish man at his workplace as well. He became good friends with this man. He was such a victim of prejudice himself and couldn't tolerate it for anyone else. It didn't matter if it was rain, sleet, or snow; he went to church. He didn't drink or smoke, except for maybe an occasional beer when my aunt and uncle came to visit. My grandfather showed us only the best example. He was generous to everyone and always supported foreign missions. He had a true Christian heart. I owe him so much. I really can't find the words to express just how much!

My grandfather was the one constant on whom my sister and I could count. When I was about five years old, I had terrible earaches. My mother was hardly ever there to take me to the doctor, and Granny just didn't do things like that, so I would cry and cry from the pain. My Granny had a thick woolen scarf from Scotland where he worked before he immigrated, and he would heat the iron and put that woolen scarf on my bad ear and iron it. It was so soothing, and the heat would penetrate deep into my ear. I know it was something he learned from his mother in Ireland. He was about seventy years old by then, and this ear pain usually hit me in the middle of the night. He would do this sometimes for an hour or more. He still worked at the golf course and got up very early, but he wouldn't ignore my pain. He was devastated that I was suffering. Eventually, my mother took me to the Marine Hospital in Baltimore. I was diagnosed with otitis media, a severe middle ear infection, and it scarred my eardrum because of the neglect. I suffered from periods of vertigo all of my life because of it, but I never forgot how much my grandfather suffered with me. I never doubted his love for Betsy and me, ever! It was just so much responsibility on him.

CHAPTER TWO

Trauma

For He has delivered me from every trouble, and
my eyes have stared down my foes.

—Psalm 54:7

My father joined the Marine Corps after the start of World War II. He was only fifteen years old. He had lied about his age and stated that he was eighteen. I just can't imagine how he had the courage to do that, but he was determined to fight for our country. My grandmother, whose name was Viola, physically went to Washington, DC, to beg for help to get him out of the service. Someone from the White House made a call to get him out, and sadly, he was on a troopship going overseas. I have read his military records that I was able to obtain from the National Archives, and it seems to validate most of what I am going to tell you now. It is very difficult to tell you all of the trauma he suffered, but I will do my best.

My father fought valiantly in World War II and in the Korean War. He was wounded three times and was awarded a Purple Heart with two clusters. He also was awarded many other medals and was invited to the White House for dinner with President Franklin Roosevelt. He had an excellent war record. I remember the following story so well. Dad and his war buddy were in a foxhole during the Battle of Okinawa, and he turned to see how his buddy was, and the boy was blown to bits right in front of his face. Daddy was fifteen years old at this time. I was five years old when he told me that story. I just wanted to cry, but I kept patting him on the shoulder and saying, "Daddy, you are so brave. You are so brave." My dad took the ring off of his buddy's finger and wore it during his entire lifetime. He also shared with me that he would carry cyanide in his pocket just in case he "was captured." I also remember how bad he felt about the use of flamethrowers during the battles. He said, "We just had to use them because the enemy was buried so deep in the holes. It was the only way to get them out." I know now as an adult that he couldn't bear to see their suffering of being burned alive. Just imagine! The sadness I felt for him was so profound, even at that tender age. I know in my heart that my father was so wounded, not only physically but also mentally. One of the wounds he received was during the Korean War. He was shot in the back after jumping off of a helicopter, and a small mortar hit him in the kidney. It made his kidney drop. He was on a hospital ship for three months. He had to be in his early twenties at that point. He went through so many battles and saw so much action. My uncle PeeWee shared with me that Dad would crawl underneath the table in my grandmother's kitchen to hide during his flashbacks. This happened just after he was home on furlough after World War II. He was in the battles of the Solomons, Saipan, Tinian, Guadalcanal, and Okinawa. He also told me that Dad was in hand-to-hand combat with the enemy. I can't imagine the terror that he went through to look into the face of the enemy like that. He saw so much, and I cannot imagine how hard that was for my dad, especially being so young.

Something I want to share with you is burned deeply into my heart. He was stationed for a brief time at the Navy Yard in Washington, DC. One day, we were driving down Constitution Avenue. As you may know, it is an extremely busy street. We were driving along, and all of a sudden, we saw a little African American boy dart across the street and was subsequently hit by a car. I was only about four, and this was before my parents had separated. My father swerved over to the side of the street and told me not to move. He ran across the street and stopped traffic as best as he could. The little boy was crying so badly. Unbelievably, the car that ran over him stripped off his little clothes. I don't know how that happened, but my father took off his jacket and put it over the little fella and held him until the ambulance got there. This was in 1957, so there were no cell phones, but thankfully, it didn't take long for them to arrive. The little boy was still crying, and Dad was cradling him and rubbing his forehead. I was jumping up and down on the front seat. I was just about hysterical, I think. Well, Dad came running back to the car and had tears streaming down his face. I said, "Daddy, is the little boy going to be all right?" My dad said, "Yes, it is going to be okay. They are going to take him straight to the hospital and then get his parents. Try not to worry." We were both crying. We didn't talk much at all after that. We were so brokenhearted. My dad just left his jacket on him as he didn't want him to be exposed like that. This incident has lived deep in my heart for sixty-some years. My father was from Virginia and was very southern, but he had no prejudice in him. I never learned to hate, and I love that little boy to this day. If by chance, you are reading this story, my little friend, I would love to know if you are "all right." I have remembered you all of my life, and I have always remembered how much you touched my father's heart too. He was not the type to cry, but he was so sad that this happened to you! My father was basically a good man, but his behavior was very hard to understand. He had such compassion that day for the little boy, but none for my mother at all. I think he not only truly hated her but also truly loved her. I just will never understand what was happening inside him. When I read his military records, it seemed that he didn't start really "acting out" until after they were married. I am wondering if he just didn't want to get married, but they had to as they were expecting me. My father had some minor infractions before his marriage but nothing serious. You will see what I mean as you continue reading.

As I mentioned, my parents separated when I was four, and my Dad very seldom came to visit us. I missed him so badly. One evening, we were upstairs sleeping. It was about midnight, and we heard a loud banging at the door. My mother ran downstairs to see who it was, and it was my dad in full military gear with trees com-

21

ing out of his helmet. I heard her screaming, "No, Tommie. No, Tommie." I was so excited, but I knew something was terribly wrong. I started to dart down the stairs and stopped in my tracks. I could see that he had a gun to my mother's head. I was only five years old and went into what I think they would call shock. I couldn't move or talk. I know my grandfather went whizzing passed me though calling out, "Tommie, Tommie, Son, come in. You are sick." Granny kept pleading with him. "Tommie, please. Son, please come in and lay down. Please give me the gun." I thought for sure that was the end of my mother and possibly my grandfather. I wanted to move, but I couldn't. Praise be to God, my father put the gun down from my mother's head and actually jumped off the porch as if he were in battle as I look back on it now, quickly got into his car, and drove off. This was just an unbelievable scene. I felt like I was watching everything in slow motion. I was amazed to see trees coming out of his helmet. I had never seen him dressed like that before. As it turned out, he was on bivouac and left to come to "kill my mother." He must have been drinking. I think I couldn't talk for two days. I never told anyone these things, so it makes me feel very sick to do so, but I know he was a casualty of war, my mother was, my sister was, I was, and so was my beloved grandfather, and this is only the beginning of that very tragic story.

My grandfather and my mother didn't stop him from coming to the house after that, however. I don't know the details, but I think my grandfather had great pity for my dad. I think he really knew he was sick and needed help. I felt so sorry for my dad. I knew he was really suffering too. He also had contracted malaria while fighting on the Islands. Sometimes, when he visited, he would lay on the couch shaking and sweating profusely. I remember hearing him say, "Sergeant, we have got to get out of here. Sergeant, Sergeant." I would just try to hold his hand and say, "Daddy, it will be okay. Please be okay." One time it was so bad, my grandfather had a doctor come to the house. The doctor said, "We really should take him to the hospital." My dad came out of it though and refused to go. He said, "I will be okay." These things are burned into my memory. Just imagine to see someone you love so much going through this and to be so little. My uncle PeeWee just recently shared with me that shortly after my father came home on furlough during the war, he was taken to the Bethesda Naval Hospital twice because his flashbacks were so severe. My father always tried to take the "Hill." My grandparents' house was located at the bottom of a hill. It was actually called the "Bottom," and he would grab a flag and a gun saying, "We've got to take the Hill." "We have got to take the Hill!" The flashbacks were horrible for him. Grandmaw was really so sad. She just didn't know what to do. It did get so bad, however, that she had someone call an ambulance, and they took him to Bethesda Naval Hospital to be treated.

One day, I was coming home from school. I was in the first grade by this time. I saw my dad's car in front of the house. Of course, I was in my glory. I just wanted to be with him all the time. I ran all the way down the street. My sister always met me after school, but she didn't that day. I just didn't know where she was. I came running up the stairs, and there was my father with his hands around my mother's neck. She was white as a sheet, and I screamed, "Daddy, Daddy, please let go. Please, Daddy, you are hurting Mommy." I couldn't get him to let go. I was out of my mind. I just took a running leap off the bed and jumped on his back. I was screaming, "You have got to let go, Daddy. Mommy is going to die. Please, Daddy. Please," and he finally let go of her neck. She fell to the floor and was white as a sheet. I thought she was dead. I didn't know what to do. I grabbed her hand, and she finally came around. I said, "Mommy, what should I do?"

She said, "Just help me up, Mary Ellen. I will be all right." Meanwhile, my father ran out of the house and jumped in his car and took off. My mother had a letter in her hand. I later found out that my father thought it was from someone she was seeing. He was insanely jealous of her, even though they were separated at that time. My mother shared that with me after she regained her senses. I was a six-year-old who was actually twenty-six. I don't know how, except through the grace of God, I was able to do what I needed to do to get him to let go of her neck. I just thank the Lord Jesus that I didn't go into shock. I just knew I had to save my mother. My mother didn't let me go to get a neighbor for help because she said, "Mary Ellen, if you get someone, they will call the police on your father." So, I said, "Okay, Mommy, I won't go. Do you want me to fix you a cup of tea?" I was out of my mind! I went outside to try to find my sister to make sure she was okay. I was really worried as I didn't know what she had seen. I finally found her hiding behind the big pine trees near the garage in the backyard. She was crying. I just grabbed her and hugged her, and I said, "Betsy, it's okay. Daddy is gone. Mommy is okay now. Please come in, and we will all have a cup of tea." And that is what we did! Being Irish, tea was our comfort! I think we drank about ten cups that day!

My mother always told me that my father wanted her dead. She was absolutely right. I thought it was the war that was making him do these things. My father admitted to the Marine Corps' base psychiatrist at Quantico that he "wanted my mother dead." He admitted that this impulse would come over him, especially if he was drinking. I could not discern what his reasons were for this after reading his service record. It was just shocking to read it. It was all true. I just can't believe that the Corps did nothing to help us. I was so proud of my father, but he was "out of his mind." He needed psychiatric help. My mother told me that the Marine Corps diagnosed him with battle fatigue and shell shock. These were the words that describe PTSD as we know it today. She told me that he had been admitted to the psychiatric ward in Bethesda Naval Hospital where I was born. This was not discernible in his service records, however. My father begged the Marine Corps to discharge him after fifteen years of service, but they would not. He told the Corps that he couldn't take it any longer. His statement in his records was, "I will make you discharge me," and eventually, he did. In my heart, I believe my father had enough of war, and Vietnam was just beginning. I have always wondered if he just couldn't go through another one. How could he take it? Who could blame him? I just don't know.

One Friday evening, my father came to visit, unannounced, and ask my mother and Granny if he could take us for the weekend. They said no and were adamant about it. I know my mother and grandfather felt so sorry for him really. I was six years old, and I wanted to spend time with him. I wanted to comfort him in any way that I could. I kept telling him how much I loved him. I begged them to let me go, and my Daddy promised to bring me back that Sunday evening. My little Betsy didn't want to go, but I pleaded with her because I told her, "Betsy, I will miss you too much! Please go with me. Daddy will be nice and it will only be for two days." So, she did. I remember Mommy and Granny asking us where he had planned to take us as they knew he was living in the barracks at the time. He said he had a family who had invited us for the weekend. I knew they weren't happy about it, but I kept begging.

So, off we go for the weekend, with a little bag packed. We pulled up to a green house in Savage, Maryland. The family who lived there was expecting us. The family consisted of a mother, a father, and three children—two boys and a girl. They were very friendly and welcoming, so I wasn't worried. I knew my father wouldn't let any harm come to Betsy or me. Well, the weekend went by, and I said, "Daddy, why aren't you taking us home. You told mommy and Granny that we would be home on Sunday." I was getting really worried. Betsy started to cry so badly. He said, "Don't worry. I am going to keep you a little longer because I haven't seen you in so long." The mother was nice enough, but I didn't like the father at all. I just really liked the two boys. I remember them vividly. The oldest boy was about sixteen, and the youngest boy was about twelve. They were so good to Betsy and me. They would take us to the park and put us on the swings because we couldn't reach them. They were so nice. One day, we were all outside having a picnic in the backyard, and all of a sudden, the boys bolted out of the house. Their father was beating them with a thick black razor strap, and I started screaming, "Daddy, please make him stop. Please, Daddy, make him stop." My heart was breaking. My father just sat there and did nothing, but he put his head down, and I could tell it was really making him feel bad. My father was not physically abusive to children at all, ever. I will never forget that scene. I will never forget those wonderful boys who were so kind to me and little Betsy. That man really hurt his children. They had welts all over them. I couldn't bear it, really. I was so upset that my father didn't stop him. It turned out that the man was an ex-Marine whom my father had known for quite a while. He was very abusive. May God forgive him. I remember going upstairs to use the restroom, and the oldest boy was in the bathtub, soaking his abused body. I yelled at him how sad I was for him and told him that I loved him, and I truly meant it.

I really wanted to get home after that, and I told Daddy, "Please take us home now. We don't want to be here anymore." Daddy kept saying, "I promise I will," but weeks kept going by, and we were still there. I know the boys were really sorry for us, and so was the daughter. I was getting to the point that I couldn't stand their parents at all. I remember the mother saying to my father, "You can stay here, but you have to buy the food. We will not feed your children." I remember her saying that so well. They were sitting on the steps in the house, and I told Daddy I was hungry. He said to me, "I will get you something to eat. Don't worry." I remember that my father started bringing groceries in after that. As it turned out, he began writing bad checks, most of which were for grocery stores. You will see that on the service record I am including in my story. Things were just terrible! I couldn't understand why my father was doing this. I believe it was about two or three months later that Betsy and I were upstairs looking out of the window and holding hands. I was telling Betsy that I think we will have to run away. I remember saying, "We will have to ask an adult to help us. We will have to run to a house if we can find one and if we can get away." All of a sudden, we saw my mother and Granny walking up the sidewalk to the house. They were accompanied by a man whom I had never seen before. He was wearing a suit. We were so excited, to say the least!

Well, Daddy came bursting into the room, with his gun in his hand, and stood at the window to get what I think would have been a good shot. I didn't go into shock. I knew I was going to do something, even if I ended up dead! I didn't care. I was going to save my mommy and my Granny. I know the gun was loaded because he opened the chamber next to my ear to check it. I felt like I wanted to go into shock, but I was determined to "fight." For some reason, he left the window where he could see them clearly and went to the doorway of the room. I think he was trying to decide what his plan of attack was going to be. He kept staring at little Betsy and me. He seemed to be in some kind of a trance His eyes were wide and blank. I said, "Daddy, Daddy, please wait. Let me go downstairs and tell them that Betsy and I want to stay with you. They have to go home. Please don't hurt them, Daddy. We just want to stay with you." I was lying, of course, but if it meant staying there to keep him from shooting them, I would have done anything. He just stood there looking at me, and I started walking toward him. I kept repeating those words: "Daddy, please give me the gun. I will go downstairs and tell Mommy and Granny and the man to go away."

I got over as close to him as possible, and I quickly tried to grab the gun out of his hand and run past him. Of course, I wasn't strong enough to get the gun, but he took one hand and picked me up and flung me across the room. He locked the door and ran downstairs. I was really hurt, but I crawled across the room to try to get to the door. I was able to hear what was being said. I heard the man who had accompanied Mommy and Granny begging my father to give him the gun. I remember him saying, "Sergeant Graves, please give me the gun. Please, Sergeant, just give me the children, and nothing will happen to you. Put the gun away. Nothing is going to happen to you. We will just drive away!" Thanks be to God, my father didn't surrender the gun, but did fly up the stairs and let us out of the room. It seemed like an eternity. The man kept begging him to let us go. Little Betsy and I jolted down the stairs and ran out of the door, into the arms of the man as fast as we could. My Granny and Mommy had been hiding in the bushes for cover down the street. Little Betsy was crying so badly. I didn't cry. I was determined to save them, no matter what it took. Once we got outside, the man said run as fast as you can. Get out of the walkway. So, we took off running, and Mommy and Granny who were waiting down the street jumped out and grabbed us as we were running. The man pulled up in his car, and we jumped in, and he drove off as fast as he could. Words just can't express how relieved we were to be with them again. My heart was so broken. Even at my age, I knew things were getting much worse for my father. My mother did tell me when we got home that the "man" was a private detective whom Granny had hired to find us. He just didn't want to call the FBI, which, in retrospect, I know would have just ended being a scene of death. My Daddy was really "losing it." As I said, when I looked into his eyes, he wasn't there. It was through the grace of our Lord Jesus that no shots were fired.

This is such a devastating story to share, and I have kept it deep inside myself for many years. I can't even express the guilt that I carried. I felt that it was all my fault because I had begged my grandfather and my mother to let me go with my dad, and then, I begged my little Betsy to go with me. If only I hadn't, I just can't tell you the trauma it caused us. I wanted to die so much, especially after that. I couldn't carry the guilt. I didn't know what to do with it. I felt so terrible leaving my father like that too. I know he was "crushed" to see us go. It was just too much to carry. He had actually been AWOL for three months according to the military records. It seemed as if we were there for an eternity. I can barely live with the memory.

After we got home, I remember that the Marine Corps starting calling my mother every day. I would listen to her to see what was going to happen to my dad. I could hear her telling them that she had not heard from him at all. Well, one day, she said to me, "Your Daddy called, and he wants to meet us downtown." I was so happy because I didn't want things to end the way they did. Betsy, Mom, and I met Dad at the local Read's Drug Store. We almost always had lunch there when we went downtown. I ran up to him and said, "Daddy, I am so glad you are okay." We are so happy to see you again." I was a little surprised that Daddy wasn't in uniform though. Well, as we left the drug store, two very nicely dressed men came up to us and said, "Sergeant Graves, we are the FBI. You must come with us." I started crying so badly. They said, "Sergeant, we will not handcuff you in front of your children. Please just come with us peacefully." He said he would, and the agents were actually very kind to him. I will never forget that scene. I did grab the coat of one of the men and begged, "Please don't take my Daddy away. Please let him stay with us. He can go to Granny's with us. It will be okay." The agent bent down, took my hand, and said, "We are going to be very nice to your Daddy. He just has to go to work now." I said, "Okay, thank you," but I was sobbing. And they just quietly walked away.

28

My mom was crying really hard too. Little Betsy was just bewildered really. I think the FBI must have been watching us in retrospect. He had been AWOL for so long, and they wanted him. It is so heart-breaking that I have nothing more to say about that.

Of course, we went back to school after we were "rescued." It was just too much for me, and I stopped eating. Sister Anne Marie asked me to have my mother come to see her because I wouldn't eat my lunch. I really did want to die. I felt responsible for all the pain I had caused my mother, father, little Betsy, and my Granny. If I hadn't been born, none of this would have happened. This is what I carried all through my life. I almost didn't survive it all but due to the mercy of our Lord Jesus.

Marine Corps

Mrs Viola Graves,
6605 Calvert Court,
Riverdale, Maryland.

The War Department
Washington D.C.

Navy

398945

Dear Sirs.

My son registered in the Marines about six months ago and gave his age as Eighteen when he is only 15 years. I realize he is too young to have that responsibility I would like very much to get him out and back home I would like to hear from you at once telling me just what to do about it I guess he just though he wanted to be with the rest of the boys in service. I am cripple and not able to get around very well and I need

(over)

30

II

him to help me. If you want to see
his birth certificate I will send it to
you. Please write soon and let me
know if I can get him out

Mrs Viola Graves
6605 Calvert Court
Riverdale Md,

31

GRAVES(898945)Tommie
E 15Oct43
Photo 10Dec43

C O P Y

UNITED STATES SENATE

July 3, 1944

Lt. Gen. Alexander A. Vandegrift
Commandant, U. S. Marine Corps
Navy Building
Washington, D. C.

Dear General Vandegrift:

     I am enclosing a letter I have received from Mrs. Viola Graves, 6605 Calvert Courts, Riverdale, Maryland, in regard to her son, Pfc. Thomas Graves of the Marine Corps, and now in the Southwest Pacific.

     You will note Mrs. Graves states her son enlisted in the Marines at the age of fifteen years, stating at the time that he was eighteen. She has been in touch with the Draft Board and has submitted his birth certificate. She is desirous of having the boy released from the service.

     I shall appreciate it if you will be kind enough to let me know what procedure she should follow in the matter and let me have the return of her letter with your reply.

     Thanking you, and with best wishes, I am

Sincerely yours,

/s/ M. E. Tydings

Enclosure

C O P Y

898945
DGN-moy

27 May 1944.

My dear Mrs. Graves:

  Your letter of recent date, regarding the underage induction of your son, Private Tommie Graves, and his present physical condition, has been received.

  As stated in Colonel Rhoads' letter of May 13, the Marine Corps reserves the right to retain or release a young man who has obtained his enlistment by misrepresenting his age or without presenting proper consent if application for his discharge is not made by his parents or legal guardian within ninety days. It is unfortunate that you did not request Private Graves' release within the specified period of time if you objected to his service; however, as he has now been in this organization seven months and is apparently performing his duties in a satisfactory manner, it would be impracticable to consider the question of his discharge at this time because of his age.

  In view of your statements regarding your son's health, I am referring a copy of your letter to his commanding officer with the request that this Headquarters be furnished a report of his present physical condition. I shall be glad to write you again when the information is received.

          Sincerely yours,

            R. M. O'TOOLE,
         Major, U. S. Marine Corps.

Mrs. Viola Graves,
 6605 Calvert Court,
  Riverdale, Maryland.

CHAPTER THREE

Court-Martial

> When fear cometh as desolation and your
> destruction cometh as a whirlwind, when trouble
> and stress overcome you.
>
> —Proverbs 1:27

As I mentioned earlier, my father started writing bad checks. They totaled about $136.00. I believe that this was during the time that he went AWOL for the ninety-nine days during which time he had "taken" us. You will see this from the military document that I am publishing here. I read that he had just passed the test for the rank of "Sergeant Major," but the Corps decided they were going to court-martial him and had planned to give him a dishonorable discharge. How devastating was this after fifteen years of great service to our country and surviving two wars! As I said, he had earned three Purple Hearts and many other citations and was also invited to the White House for a dinner honoring the Marine Corps Sixth Division of which he was a part. He fought in so many major battles in the Pacific during World War II, such as Okinawa and Guadalcanal, and many others. He had served in Korea, as well, as I mentioned earlier. My mother shared with me that my grandfather had told the Marine Corps he would cover the checks. Uncle Jimmy took her to the various stores and places where he had written them to try to "clear them up," but the Marine Corps had decided to court-martial him anyway.

As I said earlier, my father told the base psychiatrist at Quantico that he couldn't take it anymore." He asked to be discharged. He wanted my mother "dead." He admitted to that, as I have said, and that this impulse almost always happened when he was under the influence of alcohol. It is well-noted in his records that he had served our country well for fifteen years. Why did they do this? Why didn't they help my father? Why did they ignore his suffering and trauma? They wouldn't let him leave the Corps at the age of fifteen when they were sending him into battle, but they certainly were willing to let him go at the age of thirty when he was of no more use to them. Can you see the heartless cruelty in this? His defense counsel pleaded with the Corps that he be sent for rehabilitation and returned back to duty, but they refused. My grandfather and my mother were actually heartbroken for him as was my father's side of the family. My Granny wanted to help him in any way he could, but to no avail. I was six years old when he was court-martialed in 1959. I know that this broke my dad completely. He no longer knew who he was. He was no longer part of the Marine Corps, which was everything to him, but he admitted that he couldn't carry the responsibility. His trauma was just too severe. His flashbacks and malarial attacks were so pervasive in his life. I don't think he really could hold a job at that point. I truly believe that this is why his behavior was so "out of control." I don't think he would have done the things that I have told you about if he had gotten the help and the affirmation that he so needed from the Marine Corps. I cannot bear to talk about this because it still breaks my heart today as it did when I was six. I was so proud of my father, and I would like to share with you what I actually feel was the proudest moment of my life.

I was standing in line at my school when I was in the first grade. As I said, I hardly ever saw my father, but I happened to look out of the corridor door and saw this very handsome Marine, my mother, and my little Betsy standing outside waiting for me. I got so excited and yelled, 'Sister, please let me in the car line. My mother and father are here to get me!" I was so excited that I could hardly breathe. I can remember that even the Sisters who were in the corridor were so excited! They said, "Get in the car line. You have a ride home. Your dad is here," like they were shocked! I will NEVER forget that day. He was astounding with all the medals brilliantly shining in the sun. Well, sadly, the kids started to make fun of me. Some of them began saying, "We didn't know you had a father! We weren't even sure you had a mother." They were laughing and snickering at me, but I didn't care. I was holding my head up high and felt like I was six feet tall. The Sisters did tell the kids to stop or they would use the ruler. That was good because I was usually treated like a "leper" As I look back on it now, I felt like I had a big "D" on my forehead—"D" for DIVORCED. I carried that stigma but not that day. I said to them, "Shut up! My father is a MARINE, and he has been away. Who are you? Do you have a father like that? Look at all his medals, and he is so nice!" When I got outside, I ran up to him and hugged and kissed him, and some of the kids came over to meet him. It was just AWESOME. He looked like a movie star. He was very nice to them, and they treated me a little differently when I returned to school the next day. I felt a little bit like a celebrity or something. It was wonderful!

Well, I will go on because he was finally given a general discharge and kicked out like yesterday's newspaper as you can see from the papers I am including in this book. Life just got worse and worse for him and worse and worse for us too! I am so disappointed in the Marine Corps. I don't think they would have done that to him today. I hope not anyway. I do hope that I will live to see this court-martial overturned. I am going to try as hard as I can, and that is all I can say about it!

CHAPTER FOUR

House of the Dark

The Lord said he will dwell in thick darkness.
—1 Kings 8:12

I know you can just imagine how traumatized we were after going through all that with my dad, but while experiencing everything that I have just told you, so very sadly, my grandfather's house was actually haunted. Every family member who stayed in the house went through something awful, separately or collectively, except, thankfully, my sister Betsy. She always told me that she never experienced anything strange, ever. I truly thank Jesus and the Blessed Mother for that. There are so many stories to share, but I will just give you a glimpse of what we went through because it is important to the whole picture of what I am trying to share with you.

For most of us, the most terrifying experience was the noise on the stairs going up to the bedrooms. I will never forget it. Many nights, you could hear the thump—thump of the footsteps coming up the stairs to the bedrooms. It sounded like a man walking, so it was hard to tell if it was an intruder or what. One night, I remember that my uncle Jimmy spent the night, and during the middle of the night, he heard the thumping and jumped up to fight. He stood there with his fists drawn back ready to fight, and the thumping just stopped. It never failed. Everyone who heard it felt the same way. It was so real and so loud. I was standing there right next to him and could hear the thumping myself. It was terrifying!

For me and my Aunt Jane, the worse was hearing the cellar door open in the kitchen. It was so squeaky and pronounced, but my granny never went downstairs to investigate. We just don't know if he heard it or not. I began telling Aunt Jane about my experiences with all the noises and dark things when I was about five years old. She told me that she knew just what I was going through as she heard those same noises all though her childhood right through till she left to be married. There was a presence or something in the house. The kitchen seemed to be especially dark. The cellar door was in the kitchen. One night, my mom and I had been out very late. I think we had been out with Uncle Jimmy and Uncle Lou. When we came into the house, we both yelled, "Granny, there's a man in the kitchen." Mom ran up the stairs screaming, "Daddy, Daddy, help there's a man in the kitchen." I just stood there and looked. I could see him clearly. The "man" was wearing a pointy hat and just stood there staring at me, and then, he disappeared. I will never forget that night. Granny did get up to investigate, but there was nothing there. He said to us, "Oh, go ahead, Daughtas. You must be seeing things." But we weren't. I saw it, and my mother saw it. I was about five years old at that time. I thought someone had broken into the house and was waiting for us. It looked so real, and it was just unbelievable.

And of course, we had to deal with all the strange noises, tapping, and banging. Uncle Lou had stayed over one night, and he said the next morning, he heard dishes and silverware banging in the kitchen. He said it sounded like someone was setting the table. I will always remember his story. He said he called down the stairs, "Granny, is that you? Who is down there?" Of course, no one answered. He was not the kind to take things like this too seriously, but he said he was "unnerved." When he went downstairs to investigate, nothing had been moved, and the table was not set. I don't think he stayed over-night again after that—at least, that is what I remember him telling me.

My grandfather never liked to hear the stories about the "bumps in the night." I don't know why, but he would get very upset with us. One evening at dinner, however, he told my mother, Betsy, and me about something that had happened to him the night before. He said, "Daughtas, why didn't you come and help me? Didn't you hear me screaming?" We said, "No, we didn't hear anything," and he said he was terrified, but strangely, he wouldn't tell us what happened to him. He said it was too terrible to talk about. We felt so badly that we didn't run to help him. It was all just so sad and so overwhelming! He never shared what happened to him during his whole lifetime. I just can't imagine what he saw.

I remember I tried not to look at the doorway of the middle room where Mom, Betsy, and I slept. So many times, I saw the form of a "man" just standing there. My heart felt as if it was going to explode. I want to share with you the most terrifying night of my life as far as the paranormal goes that is. The night seemed to be especially dark. I had such a terrible feeling. I heard the "thump, thump, thump" coming up the stairs. As I said, it always sounded like a man's footsteps, and it would stop at the last step. Well, I looked over at the doorway, of our room, and I actually saw a figure of a bear standing straight up but with a very scary face. I just was too afraid to move. The "bear" came walking into my room and came over to my bed. All I knew to do was to turn away from it. I turned on my left side as I had my back to it for fear that it would scratch me or bite me. I could feel its hair on my face, and it began sniffing my face and my ear. I could feel its breath. I could smell a bad odor. In my heart, something kept telling me not to move. I was praying silently and kept my eyes shut tight so the "thing" would think I was asleep. Thank the Lord Jesus, it finally left my room. I heard it walking down the stairs. I know this is absolutely unbelievable, but please keep an open mind as you will see that this truly happened to me. I quickly jumped out of bed and ran into my grandfather's room and got into bed with him. There was a large crucifix of our Lord over Granny's bed, so I knew I would be safe somehow. I never shared this story with anyone, not even my Aunt Jane. I was only about six years old when this happened, and I believe it came shortly after my dear little friend, Dana, died. I really feel that the day Dana died was the day I wanted to die too!

Granny always prayed with us before we went to bed, and he came around with the holy water and blessed us and the doorways to the bedrooms and the stairwell. My Aunt Jane told me that when they were young, Granny had the house blessed twice by a priest. Sadly, it didn't stop the activity. We just all learned to live with it the best way we could, but it was hard, to say the least.

Life went on, and things just got more and more dark and more and more sad as you will see.

CHAPTER FIVE

Abandonment

The sacrifices of God are a broken spirit: a broken and a contrite heart, Oh God, thou will not despise.

—Psalm 51:17

It was 1962. I remember it well because this happened during the Cuban Missile Crisis. As some of you may remember, we had to have drills at school and go underneath our desks or go down into the basement when the siren began to blare. I really wanted to be with my father. I just didn't know where he was. It was a very scary time for everyone. Even the nuns were nervous. After my father's court-martial, he was so lost and flat broke. He didn't know what to do with his life. It came over the radio that Tommie Graves and an accomplice had been arrested in Virginia for attempted robbery of a gas station. Uncle Gene had heard it while he was traveling and quickly called my mother. Everyone in the family was very embarrassed to hear it. I, on the other hand, was devastated, and so was my grandfather. My father received a year in a state penitentiary in Virginia. He had gotten in touch with my mother to see if his cellmate's wife would be able to bring me to see him. He and his cellmate had become good friends. I begged my mother to let me go to see him. I was about nine years old at the time. I remember that my mother had dressed me to the "nines." I looked like a "Kennedy kid" as people used to say in those days. I went with the lady, and she walked in a little ahead of me. I looked around and saw all the state troopers with shotguns in the upper level, and I just fainted straight out. When I awoke, a state trooper was holding me. He was very upset. He said to the lady, "Why did you bring this innocent child here? She is way too young to see this." I begged him, "Please I want to see my Daddy. Please." He gave me to the lady, and she held me by the arm and walked me over to the window where the phones were, and when they brought my father out, he was handcuffed. They took him out of the handcuffs and brought him over to the window where I was. I just couldn't take it. He looked so scared and so depressed. Sadly, I lost my ability to speak. I just kept putting my hand on the window to try to reach out and touch him. He put his hand up so my hand would match his, and we just kept looking at each other through the glass. I tried so hard to talk, but I couldn't. Tears were just rolling down my cheeks. I wanted to say, "Daddy, I am so sorry for you. I love you so much," but I couldn't. I felt like I would just die of a broken heart right there on the spot. As I remember, I regained my speech in about two days. I have never recovered completely from any of this. It is just too painful to remember.

My life changed forever in 1963. My mother told me that my father was to be released soon from prison and that she was very afraid. She actually told me she was "afraid that he intended to kill her." I don't know if he had told her that in his letters from prison, but I know that is how she really felt. I said, "Mommy, it will be okay. I will never leave you. He won't hurt you with me around." Usually, she would be away for maybe a week or two at a time, but this time three weeks went by and then four, five, then six weeks. Uncle Jimmy and Uncle Lou became very concerned as we all were, and while Granny was at the golf course working, they called the state police to report her missing. I was terrified that she was dead. My grandfather got off early from the golf course that day because of the bad weather. He came limping up the street as fast as he could. He was so upset as he thought that either Betsy or I was hit by a car. He was so upset with Uncle Jimmy for calling them. He told the state trooper to please leave his house. He was not needed. The trooper was very upset, but I remember him like yesterday. He told Granny, "You need to file a report. Something has happened to your daughter. No one has heard from her in six weeks, and she has two children here. Who is taking care of them?" Granny said, "I am. You don't need to worry just go," and he did. The trooper was very upset, to say the least. I will never forget it. I was ten years old at this time. So, Betsy and I were just taking care of ourselves as we always did, but this situation was much worse than usual in that regard. Our clothes were stained, and we didn't have any underwear, and Granny just didn't know how to take care of us. Betsy and I went to school in "bad shape" really. We had school uniforms of course, but they were unclean, and we didn't have anything else to wear to school. Granny always left us two dollars on top of the radio in the kitchen before he left for work at 6:00 a.m. That was a lot of money back then. We could go to the movies and get candy for dinner until Granny came home from work. One day, my teacher, who was really a wonderful person, took me out in the hall and told me as kindly as possible that she was giving me deodorant and a training bra as I was starting to develop at that early age. She asked me, "Where is your mother? Why aren't you being taken care of?" I just started to cry, which I hardly ever did, and I told her that my mother was missing. She hugged me and told me to make sure that I wore the bra and used the deodorant that she gave me. I thanked her and went back to my seat and just wanted to disappear! It was maybe about two months later that my mother finally called and told us that she had remarried and that she wouldn't be back. My father had been released from prison, and he came directly to see Betsy and me. He had no idea mom was gone. I begged him, "Daddy, if you don't take care of us, the state is going to take us away and put us in foster homes." I don't know who called social services, and I have never been able to find out, but they came and made my Granny sign a paper. He had a third-grade education and was not sure what he had signed. It was a form relinquishing custody of Betsy and me. He was "flattened." Grandmaw and Grandpaw Graves wanted to take us, but the state told Granny that they were too poor. It was devastating to hear, that but I told my father, "You have got to take care of us." He took us to Montgomery Ward and bought two dresses for little Betsy and also two for me and some underwear. It must have been money he earned while in prison. It was an awesome feeling! I was so very happy! When he was leaving that day, he promised me, "I will be back tomorrow to get you and to see Granny to let him know." I truly believed him. I waited and waited, and he never came back. I went out on the porch every day and looked for him and waited and nothing. I knew we were going to be taken away. I just couldn't believe that he didn't love us—that he didn't care that we would be put in foster homes. I cannot express the betrayal that I felt! Granny was so crushed because they were going to put Betsy in one home and me in another. Granny called various Catholic boarding schools, but we were turned away because of being children of divorce. I could hear him talking to the schools on the phone, and after he hung up, he would cry and cry. I would go to him and hug him and say, "Granny, Betsy and I don't want to leave you." It was just DEVASTATING. Thank our Lord Jesus, my Aunt Jane and Uncle Gene decided to take us as long as Granny was willing to pay for our support and to have an extra bedroom added to their house. They had three children at that time, and I know it was very difficult to take on two more. As I said, by the time this happened, Betsy was nine years old, and I was ten. The state told my grandfather that a court date had been scheduled at the Maryland Department of Juvenile Services in Baltimore. Of course, Betsy and I had to sit in the front row with my Aunt Jane and Uncle Gene beside us. My mother and father were summoned as well, and my mother came, but my father never showed. I remember this like yesterday. The judge said to my mother, "You really don't want your children any longer?" My mother said, "No, I don't." The judge was overwhelmed. He just couldn't believe it! I don't know why the state put my little Betsy and me there to hear just how much we weren't wanted. I really thought I never was wanted anyway, but to hear that said was the "end of me." I think Betsy thought that way too, but we really didn't talk about this kind of stuff till we were in our teens. My mother did tell my Aunt Jane that her new husband didn't want us, so she had no choice. I can understand now in many ways

45

why she abandoned us so completely because she was terrified of my father, and I think she felt she had to do something in order to save her life. She thought being married to this guy would do it. He was an ex-Marine, and I think she felt safe because of that. Boy was she wrong, but that is a whole other story!

I can still remember watching Granny cry as we pulled away. My friends Theresa and Kathy were there, as well, to say goodbye to us. My heart was wrenching. I didn't know how I was going to go on without my granny. Leaving him was just too sad! I didn't want to leave any of them at all. My little friend Theresa's face was white as a sheet, and her big blue eyes were so sad, as were Kathy's. I watched as little Theresa and Kathy just stood there stunned as we pulled away. My grandfather's heart was breaking, and he was crying so hard as he just stood at the top of the street with my little friends watching us leave. I just wanted to jump out of the car. It is burned in my memory and in my heart. Betsy and I cried all the way to Norfolk, Virginia, which took eight hours at that time. I really didn't want to go on anymore at all. Life had just been too sad.

I loved my aunt and uncle, and I loved my cousins, and I am very grateful to them for their generosity for taking us and caring for us. I would have lost my sister, too, had they not taken us. She would have been in one foster, and I would have been in another. I doubt very much that the state would have tried to let us see each other or to see my Granny either. As I said, my aunt and uncle had three children of their own, and I know it couldn't have been easy for them. My aunt was a very devout Catholic. She was a terrific person. I don't think I really understood exactly how terrific she was until I was much older. Shortly after Betsy and I went to live with them, Aunt Jane became pregnant with her fourth child. Her name is Patty, and she was and is the sweetest little thing. She would come down to our room and whisper in my ear when she was about two years old and say, "Mary Ellen, I love you." My cousins treated us like we were sisters. It was so great to have all of their love and support, and Aunt Jane and Uncle Gene did their very best for us.

It is just so hard to talk about, but I could hardly bear all that I had been through. I couldn't bear the devastation that I felt being abandoned by my mother and father and having to leave behind my grandfather and my little friends whom I loved too. I knew I wouldn't see my Grandmaw and Grandpaw Graves again either and all my dad's brother and sister whom I loved so much too. I don't think my Aunt Jane and Uncle Gene realized how devastating losing my family was to me. I think Betsy was very happy there, but I was crushed. I wanted to be with my granny and my mother. I wanted to see my father again, my Grandmaw and Grandpaw, and aunts and uncles to whom I had grown so close and, of course, Uncle Jimmy and Uncle Lou too. They did come to visit us sometimes! It was always wonderful to see them!

All along, I did have a deep faith in our Lord Jesus, and my plan in life was to serve Him. I tried to go on as best I could. I tried so hard to hide my sadness. Sister Robert used to keep me after school because she knew how much I missed my mother and my granny. I don't know how she figured all this out, but she knew things were very hard for me. I told Sister that I wanted to become a nun, and she thought I would have been a good one. She thought a lot of me, and that meant so much. I told my aunt that I had the desire to become a nun, and she was very encouraging. She had arranged for me to work for the Sisters of Charity at the local Catholic hospital. Even though she was caring for six children, she drove me every Saturday without fail to work. It was more or less arranged that I would enter this order when I turned sixteen, but as you will see, this never happened. Oh God, how I wish that it did!

Uncle Gene told my mother that it was time for her to take Betsy and me back to live with her. He had four children and was trying to give my mother the opportunity to get her life together. She was working in a bar, and the people at the bar really loved her and treated her more like a family. She made good money there, and I guess her husband had relented. I don't know why as it turned out to be the worst nightmare ever!

So, we left Aunt Jane's in 1967. Betsy was thirteen, and I was fourteen. Betsy didn't want to leave at all. She loved it there. She had so many friends and was very popular. I missed my mother so much and was glad to be with her again. I want to say that my aunt was so good to us. She never showed favoritism, and my sister and I always had the same things that my cousins had. I loved them all so much, but I wanted to get back to my mother and father. My father did call my Aunt Jane to see if he could visit us while we lived there. She did let him come, and I was so very happy to see him again. He was in his early forties and had brought his fiancée with him. She was very nice, and I liked her. I was so hoping that our lives would go on together, but they didn't. It all turned out to be so sad.

I could never imagine that I would turn away from my faith so completely. I could never imagine that I would hurt my grandfather so much. I know that he said the rosary for me every day. My grandfather was my compass, and I don't think I would be alive today if it weren't for him and the love of my little Betsy. Well, the story goes darker sadly.

CHAPTERS SIX

Hell Never Ended

The Lord is my helper. Therefore, I will look in triumph on those who hate me.

Psalm 118:7

I remember so well the day my mother and her new husband came to Norfolk to bring us back to Maryland. His name was Dicky, and he seemed to be very nice. He was a little younger than my mother and was a very nice-looking, educated man. He had attended Penn State, and his mother and father were teachers. I thought maybe, things were going to work out. I remember when my mom went into our bedroom to change her sweater before we left Norfolk; her ribs were wrapped in white tape all the way around her. I asked her what happened, and she said she had hurt her back at work. I felt so bad for her. She was a very petite woman as I mentioned, so I thought this must have really hurt her. So, off we went. My Aunt Jane was very sad to see us go, and she was standing at the door crying as we pulled off. Betsy was very sad too, and I felt so bad about it.

My mother had rented a townhouse in Laurel, Maryland. Our bedroom was very nice, and the house was furnished very nicely too. My stepfather was a real history buff, and we had all kinds of souvenirs. I loved history myself, so I was very fascinated by some of the things he had acquired. He was really funny, and he made us laugh so much! I thought, "Well, this is all going to work out." I was going to my first year of high school at a very prestigious Catholic high school in Laurel. It was very well-known and highly respected. My sister was to attend Laurel Middle School until the following year, and then, she would be going to my high school with me. I was so looking forward to that. I didn't like to be anywhere without my sister. I couldn't stand life without her.

Well, as it turned out, my stepfather was a stone-cold drunk and was the meanest, cruelest person I had ever met. My mother admitted to me that her back was wrapped because he had beaten her so badly that he cracked her ribs. He would come home so "loaded" after a night of drinking at the local bar and try to hurt my mother. You could hear his car coming "put-putting" down the road, and my heart would just start to race, and Betsy and I would put ourselves into a fighting mode. My mother would come into our room, jump in bed with us so we could protect her, and we did! My sister was very physically strong, and I was not, but I was very determined as you know. One of the worst things he tried to do was to come into our room and throw my mother off of the bed, of course, with us on it, and pour food on her head and on us. He was totally disgusting! May God have mercy on him! My sister would grab one side of him, and I would grab the other, and we threw him out of the room as hard as we could and lock the door. We lived in a duplex, and our neighbors were all very "cool" guys in their twenties. I used to "pray to God" that they would come and help us, but they never did. They were so upset by all of this though, and the police were called almost every night, and I am not exaggerating! Once again, we were the talk of the neighborhood and the town. The violence only got worse with him, and eventually, he began to attack my Betsy and me. I went to school one day after such a violent attack the night before, and Sister asked me to stay after school as she wanted to talk to me. She asked me, "Why do you look so bad? What has happened to you?" She was from Germany and had survived the Nazis. She was very upset and actually started to cry. She asked me if there was anything she could do to help me. I wouldn't answer her. I just said, "Please, Sister, don't cry. I will be okay. Please don't worry about me," and she let me go home.

Well, that day, I was on my way home and looked like "hell itself," and in front of our house was a limousine with the words "Grand Imperial Wizard" and underneath "KKK." I was just out of mind with anger. I knew all about that organization. I hated them! I went into the house with my Catholic school uniform and my fighting mode and told him to "GET OUT. What are you doing here? JUST GET OUT! YOU ARE EVIL!" Dicky was there and couldn't believe I did this. The Wizard just looked so shocked and hurt really and got up and left. He didn't say a word to my stepfather. I told my stepfather, "If you put a hand on me, YOU WILL BE SORRY!" I walked down to his parents' house and told them because I knew how good these people were. They were just appalled and sickened. They got in the car and came up to the house. His dad asked me to stay outside while he handled this, and I did. Dicky NEVER said a word to me about it, EVER! Thank God, I never saw that Wizard again!

The attacks just got so bad though that my little Betsy had ENOUGH! Betsy decided to go back to Catonsville to live with my Granny. She had made this decision because one night, Dicky came barging into our room after breaking the lock. Betsy and I grabbed him and try to throw him out, but somehow, he got a hold of Betsy and tried to throw her out of the window. I was fighting as hard as I could. I grabbed my purse and started beating him with it, and finally, Betsy and I were able to get him down on the ground. The police were at the door, and I screamed for help, and they burst through the door! They were going to arrest him, but my mother wouldn't let them, and they didn't. How do you explain that? I will never understand it, never. I really wanted to go back to Catonsville with my sister, but I said, "Betsy, if we leave mom here alone with him, he will kill her." Betsy agreed. It was so sad. I couldn't stand being separated from her. I never shared this with my sister, but I knew I couldn't go back to Granny's house to live. I was terrified of the "bear." I was terrified of all the thumping on the steps and the cellar door opening for no reason and always during the nighttime. I couldn't have taken that anymore either, so I just had to stay. I wasn't as strong as Betsy as

I said, but I learned how to push him and knock him down because he was always so drunk. One day, after a particularly hateful night, I decided that I would kill him. He had made a sexual advance to me the night before. I was so disgusted. May God forgive me. He had come home rather early the following night, and instead of coming upstairs and "starting," he just went to sleep on the couch. We had a huge red ashtray on the coffee table, and I just lost it. I quietly went downstairs to make sure he was good and drunk. He was passed out. I picked up the ashtray and was just ready to bash his head in with it, and thanks be to Jesus, my mother opened the front door just as I had it over my head to "finish him." I will never forget that as long as I live. She screamed, "Mary Ellen, please don't. Please don't." Thank God, she did. I think I wouldn't have stopped beating him until he was dead. The hatred and anger that ran through me were just overwhelming. I was only fifteen, but I had enough of suffering. I just couldn't take it anymore. I NEVER understood why she tolerated him and why she didn't leave him. I don't think she had my father to fear any longer because he had a new wife. I think he changed quite a bit after going through the humiliation of being in prison. This man was way more to be feared than my father at that time. I was trying to find my dad because I was going to beg him to beat the "hell" out of this man. I was going to tell my father everything! This man was a coward, and I think he would have left us if he had to deal with my father. I think that would have solved everything, but unfortunately, I didn't find my dad until it was just too late!

Finally, my mother met another man and decided it was time to divorce this monster. I was so relieved. I called Betsy and begged her to come back to Laurel because I was so lonely without her. She wanted to stay at her school, and she had a lot of friends there, so I completely understood how she felt. She was okay, and most importantly, she was with our Granny.

So, my mother and my new stepfather got married, and we moved to a very nice apartment in Laurel. His name was Billy Sullivan, but he was called "Sully." He was a great man and had been through seven campaigns during World War II and survived. I was sixteen then, and it was such a relief to be rid of the "monster." Sully and I used to talk about his war experiences almost every night after dinner. It was wonderful not to be under that kind of nightly stress of abuse and hatred. I was actually starting to enjoy life a little bit, and I think Betsy was as well.

One evening, my mother and Sully went to a function at the local fire department. Dicky was there with his new wife and talked to my mother. He asked her to tell Betsy and me how very sorry he was for the way he treated us and that he hoped we would forgive him. I am not really sure how Betsy felt, but I wasn't about to forgive him. It was only through the grace of God that eventually, I was able to do so. I can't tell you how many years that took really. I am very grateful for that because our Lord says that we must forgive in order to be forgiven, and as you will see, I have been forgiven so much!

I began to meet a lot of people at Laurel High School and was becoming fairly popular. I was still a "good girl," but I got into some hard drinking. I had been through so many "wars" myself as had my sister, so sadly drinking became my way to deal with it all.

I was still trying to find my father, though. I don't remember how it all came about, but I think my Aunt Julie had been able to arrange it. She lived in Laurel too, and I think she had seen him. If I remember correctly, he and his new wife had started a new business on Main Street. Aunt Julie came to my house to talk to my mother and Sully to make sure it was okay with them if my father came to our apartment. So, it was arranged. I remember it was a little awkward because I think Sully was uneasy. That day, Dad and I had arranged for Betsy and me to come to dinner at his house to see his wife, Ronnie, and meet his stepchildren and his grandson. I was excited to go, and I called Betsy that evening, but she was reticent. She thought it over and decided to go with me. We had a very nice evening, but Betsy and I were both kind of distant from Dad and his new family, as I remember. We hadn't seen my father in about six years, and we had been through a lot, as you know, and didn't feel as though we really knew him.

I wanted to get to know Dad again, and I really liked Ronnie. She had two sons who were really nice and very protective of Betsy and me. They were both in their twenties. I wasn't used to that at all.

53

I was kind of flattered by the attention really. I could tell that Dad didn't feel physically well at all. I think he was only about forty-eight at the time. While we were having dinner, he began to perspire profusely, but he did not have the shakes as he did during an attack of malaria. I remember feeling very worried about him and very sorry for him.

I feel so sad talking about this because it will hurt me until I leave this world. I was working part-time in the evenings. My new stepfather always took me to work and picked me up. I really appreciated that. I saw my father periodically and began to feel closer to him. He always put his arm around my waist, and I found it to be comforting because I remembered him doing that when I was little. He was actually a very kind man in many ways. He also had a great sense of humor and made me laugh, and I remember that as a child as well. One day, I asked Dad if he would consider buying me a used car. I told him I would pay for the payments and the insurance, but I just didn't have enough for a down payment. I didn't want to ask my grandfather because he had done enough for me, and Sully had my mom quit work after they married. Dad was actually struggling financially because he and Ronnie had just started the new business, but I believe Ronnie decided to do it. I remember they had to put $400.00 down on a 1966 Malibu Convertible. It was really nice! My payments were $50.00 a month, and I worked every day after school to keep things going. Well, one day, I made a very bad mistake. My car needed a repair, and I knew the owners of the gas station very well where I was going to leave it overnight. A boy from my class worked there, and I remember saying to him, "If you need to drive it, I am sure it will be okay." I actually meant to say if you need to drive it to see how it is running, but this boy took it out and got totally drunk and totaled it. It is a true miracle that he wasn't killed. My dad and I went to see it the next day, and it was totally mangled. I was just devastated, and so was my dad. The owners told my dad that they had nothing to do with it as the boy came on the lot in the middle of the night and took it out. They wouldn't take any responsibility at all because they said I had given the boy permission to drive it. It was all such a nightmare. Well, to make a long story short, my father called me a couple of days later and told me that I had to keep making the payments. I didn't understand that and still don't till this day, but my sister kept telling me, "Just forget it. Dad is just trying to use you." Dad and I had a huge argument, and we never spoke again. I can barely write about this.

I know this is going to sound strange, but one evening, I was in my room alone, and I felt a presence. I was told somewhere in my heart, at least three times, "You must call your father. You must call your father. You must call your father." I couldn't see the presence, but I could feel it. It is really hard to describe, but I felt the urgency of the message and decided to do it. I was trying hard to get up my courage, and finally, about a week later, I picked up the phone and called him. When I heard dad's voice, I panicked and hung up. About a week later, I was with my sister, and she got a call from my Aunt Julie, and Betsy put me on the phone. Aunt Julie said, "Your father died last night." My head starting swimming, and I just wanted to scream out, but I couldn't. I was DEVASTATED because I could have talked to him before he died. The heavenly being warned me to call him. I wanted to call and say how sorry I was for all the misunderstanding and that I really loved him and wanted to see him again. If only I had the chance! My heart was and is broken to this day. As an aside, I think my father knew he was going to die. My mother and Sully told me that they thought for sure he was at the farm where Sully had kept his horse. They saw someone walking up the side road and thought for sure it was him. My mother said our German shepherd was barking so ferociously that Dad turned around and walked back to his car and drove off. My father was a dog handler during the war, so I am sure he understood German shepherds well and knew it was just too risky. My mother was sure that Dad wanted to see us again before his death. I truly believe that too, because the night when he died, I was standing in the living room and all of a sudden I felt someone put their arm around my waist. I thought it was my sister just goofing around, and I turned quickly around, and there was no one there. I just know it was my dad saying goodbye to me. I pray to our Lord that it was. As I said, I didn't know he had died until the next morning.

I remember I was so sad and felt such horrible guilt. Sully let me drive his truck to Catonsville to see Granny. My Granny was terribly sorry that Dad had died. I know he had a lot of feelings for him and compassion. Granny and I sat on the porch holding hands and crying. He kept saying, "Daughta, I am sure that your father is okay. Please try not to worry. I will keep him in my prayers always. He didn't mean to do the things he did."

My stepmother tried so hard to get the Marine Corps to give my dad a military funeral, but they declined. She was so devastated. I remember when Betsy and I went to the funeral home to see him, I fainted. My stepmother came running over to me as I was coming around and hugged me. That meant a lot to me as I know I really hurt my father. I hated myself so much for that. I will never forget that the funeral procession had to pass our apartment on the way to the cemetery. My mother and Betsy's little son, Sean, who was five at the time, were standing outside to say goodbye to him. Little Sean was standing there very erect and saluting him as the procession drove by. Betsy and I were so proud of him. My mother was crying very hard and waved. I always felt that she never really stopped loving my father. It was all so terribly sad.

I never saw my stepmother again or her family. My uncle Bob and I always go to the cemetery where Dad is buried with my flags and flowers. Sadly, one day, we went, and my stepmother was buried next to Dad. Coincidentally, my sister and Ronnie were both born on September 10. I didn't know that. The headstone said, "Finally together forever." I just broke down and cried and cried.

CHAPTER SEVEN

Adoption

For the wrath of God is revealed from heaven against all ungodliness and unrighteousness of men, who by their unrighteousness suppress the truth.

—Romans 1:18

I always thought that I was so unattractive. After I went through the awkward stage at about fourteen, people started telling me I was pretty. Well, I was "off and running," so sadly, I decided to leave my Catholic high school and went to the public high school. I wasn't used to being noticed at all, but I was becoming fairly popular and was becoming fairly "wild." I got into the so-called "cool" crowd and started drinking very heavily, as I said before. I was bringing liquor to school when I was a junior and a senior. As you know, my life had been very hard, so I just escaped through booze and partying. I do not, however, mean to blame my decisions in life on anyone but myself. I am totally responsible for my very bad decisions. After I graduated, which was a real struggle, as I was always being suspended for "cutting school," I worked in various department stores while I attended community college majoring in secretarial science. In 1973, I got my first clerical job in Washington, DC. I was nineteen, and I thought life was just great! It was a very exciting time, and I loved working there. I met so many wonderful and interesting people, and they really seemed to like me. It was the most wonderful feeling, as I grew up feeling so unwanted and unaccepted. I usually attended Mass at lunchtime at St. Matthew's Cathedral, and I know that I loved God, but I turned away from everything that I knew to be right and true. I turned away from everything I was taught. Jesus asks us in the Bible not to have sex before marriage. I wish I had listened to Him as you will see.

Sadly, I became pregnant in 1976. I was twenty-two years old, and my "boyfriend" did not want anything to do with me or the baby. I was determined to have it, even though abortion was legal, so I decided to go to a Catholic home for unwed mothers in Washington, DC. It was such a devastating feeling to be so rejected once again, but I went to Mass every morning, which I found very comforting even though I had really not given God much thought. The nun who took care of us was very kind, and the priest who came to the home was so caring. I felt a strange kind of peace, but I truly thought Jesus would send my baby's father to find me and marry me and bring me and my baby home. I was somehow convinced that I wouldn't have to give my baby up for adoption in the end. I didn't want to do it, but I knew that I was somehow defective and a partyer, and I didn't trust myself to raise a child by myself, not to mention that I was terrified that I would give my baby the same kind of childhood I had.

I had a natural delivery because I had developed severe toxemia. I remember saying to the doctor while I was in labor, "Do you think my baby will forgive me?" I said it over and over again. He was actually crying. It was such a crushing experience to know that I would never be able to hold my child. My little baby boy was in the nursery on the same floor, and I was able to walk down the hall to see him through the glass. I was not able to hold him, though. I could hear the nurses saying, "How can she give up her baby? What kind of person is she?" It was so cruel. He was so beautiful. Just perfect! Words just can't express the devastation, so I won't even try. My sister was with me when we left the hospital. My son was actually in the elevator with us. My social worker had him in her arms. I don't know why they allowed that to happen, but my sister wanted to grab him and run. I said, "No, Betsy, I know this is the right thing for him," but I could barely stand up.

When the social worker went the opposite way with my baby, I left the hospital doubled over. I just wanted to die! Deep in my heart, though, I felt it was truly the right thing to do. His life was too precious to me to take the chance of raising him. I knew I was defective, and I was so afraid I wouldn't give him a good life.

I was able to pick out his family with my social worker, who was a very compassionate person and helped me a lot. So, I was totally involved in his aftercare and in his placement with his adoptive family. I picked out a family that had no natural children of their own. I was adamant about that. They were Catholic, of course, and were very well-educated and successful. I had two months to change my mind if I decided not to go through with the adoption. But something inside of me said, "No, this is right for him."

Well, the day came when it was time to sign the final adoption papers. I felt that I could barely stand up. My head was swimming. Sadly enough, the date was February 23, and my father had died that very day a year before. I was so wishing he could be with me. He had been adopted, and I wanted to ask him what to do. I tell you this because I don't mean to say that adoption is easy. It was for me a very devastating, life-changing experience, but a child's life is so precious, and I think it is so important to make sure that a child grows up with security and love, not to mention stability. I believe that we cannot use children to fix what is wrong with ourselves, and I think so many women do that. It is so wrong because the child usually pays in the end, and I wasn't going to let that happen to my son!

I was so sad that the only thing I could think to do was to go back to work as soon as my stitches were out, which I did. I was interviewing two weeks after I left the hospital. I tried to go on as if nothing was wrong. I had gotten a very good secretarial job in DC, but I was a mess. I cried all the time, mostly at lunchtime. My boss noticed that something was wrong, so I decided that perhaps, the best thing to do was to get a less stressful job with a less stressful commute, which was an hour each way. I was so hoping that it would help, but it didn't, as you will see.

CHAPTER EIGHT

Abortions

What is done in secret will come to light...
—Luke 8:17

After I left DC, I got a very good job with my local government. I know that God must have been looking out for me even then, because I was very well thought of there. I loved my boss and the people I worked with, and I think working there kept me going, for a time anyway. I subsequently moved into a very nice high-rise apartment that was near to my work, and I thought I would be okay. Well, I couldn't have been more wrong.

I was drinking very heavily and partying. I met a man, whom I loved very much, but I didn't trust anyone after my son's father, and most of all, I didn't trust myself. We had been dating for some time, and a friend of his came to the kitchen at his house and sat to talk with me. He told me that my boyfriend had actually met someone else. My boyfriend hadn't told me anything about her, but I could feel him pulling away from me. I was devastated because, sadly, once again, I found myself pregnant. I decided to take off for Arizona to visit two of my cousins who moved there from Virginia. I wanted to get away to try to figure out what I was going to do. I didn't even share it with them that I was pregnant. I got so sick on the plane, and they had to have a wheelchair for me when we landed. Well, when I came back, I had decided I was going to tell him. I was having a lot of pain on my left side, and it was difficult for me to work. I think he thought I was "lazy." He couldn't have been more wrong about me, because I was sick. I wasn't going to take the chance of telling him that I was pregnant, because I just knew he would reject me, so I decided to have an abortion. He wasn't the kind of man who would have rejected the baby, but I didn't want to be alone again. I just couldn't take it! I didn't trust myself to raise a child alone as I have said before. I know he would have helped to support the child, but I was too damaged! I had a very good friend, who told me about a doctor in DC who performed abortions (I don't remember why we couldn't get one done in Maryland at the time), and so, I made an appointment. The abortionist's office was in a small brownstone building on "D" Street in Northwest DC. It looked like any other doctor's office would. I was scared to death. The doctor was an older man and was actually very kind. I don't know why he was in that business, and it still puzzles me to this day. It was very early in the pregnancy, so I just kind of thought of it like a D&C. I don't think I really thought of it as a human baby until after the procedure, when the doctor asked me if I wanted him to baptize the baby. I said, "Yes," and we went down to the basement. What a dichotomy! So, there, he and I were with the little embryo in a container saying prayers while he baptized the baby with holy water. To tell you, this is so crushing because obviously he and I must have realized that it was a true human life that we had taken. I wouldn't let myself think about it. I went home and lay on the floor for a while; I was in some pain as the procedure itself was very painful, but then, I couldn't take the sadness so I got dressed and called my friend, and off, we went to the bar. I got smashed as I usually did, but I couldn't deal with what I had done, so I didn't. I just stuffed it away and went on, or so I thought. I have never gotten over the loss of that relationship or the loss of my baby. It has always been a pain in my heart. Strangely, I didn't give God a second thought though, because I don't think I cared; after all, I felt that God had let me down when I didn't get my "miracle" about my son. I felt like God didn't care for me, so why should I worry about what He thought?

Just when it seemed that I couldn't sink any lower, I found myself pregnant again. I was actually dating someone whom I had no feelings for at all. I felt a lot safer about it that way. I knew he couldn't possibly hurt me. I went to the same doctor and had another abortion. We baptized this baby too. This time, though, something really died inside of me. I was cold. I don't think I grieved at all. It was the easy way out, and I took it. After all, I felt that my son's adoption was killing me and the loss of my relationship and baby who meant so much to me was killing me, so nothing could be worse than that, or so I thought. So, once again, I pushed it way down inside of me, and I didn't speak of it to anyone except for my best friend. I'm not even sure if I told my sister.

All this time, a self-hatred was brewing in me that I can never truly explain, and as you know, it had been brewing since childhood. I just drank more and more and partied more and more. My sister married young and had two children. I did love my sister's children very much, but I would never let myself think of having a husband and children after that. I think I would have committed suicide if I didn't really believe that there was a God somewhere. I knew there was a God, but I was really "mad" at Him, and I didn't want anything to do with Him. I told our Lord that I was "Done with Him!" I believe that I totally opened my soul up to the devil that day. I didn't know much about the devil or his power, but I was soon to find out!

CHAPTER NINE

The Apartment and the Dark

For we do not wrestle against flesh and blood,
but against principalities, against powers, against
the rulers of the darkness of this world.
                                    —Ephesians 6:12

As I mentioned earlier, I was living in a very nice high-rise apartment during the time that I had these abortions. For some reason, I was scared to death in that apartment. I don't know why exactly, but I could never really sleep well.

I was extremely lonely and, as I said, terribly frightened, but I didn't know why. I began to feel that I wasn't alone in the apartment sometimes. Things felt darker and darker to me, but I was a drinker and "partyer" and had a good job and looked on the surface like everything was okay. I took a long break from men, though. I just went out with my friends and drank and drank. I didn't walk around acting miserable, I think. I just tried to have fun, and I did have fun. My good friend and I went to all the best places (she was still working in DC at the time), and we met interesting people, but the hole that was inside of me was growing deeper and deeper. I thought about my son all the time. I missed him terribly, but I remember thinking what kind of mother would I be if I'm always out drinking and partying. "I never really had a mother or a father." Well, I digress. Eventually,

I did meet a very nice man. He was an undercover policeman at the time, and I think I liked that because I was afraid, but I wasn't sure why. I felt safe with him, and he treated me very well. He was extremely intelligent, and I valued his opinion. I sort of felt that if he liked me, I must not be so bad. I was very emotionally dependent on him, though, but I don't think I showed it. I'm not sure if he knew that. I hope not anyway!

Well, we didn't live together, but I liked it when he spent the night. He was always on assignment as I remember, so that wasn't very often. One night, I was lying on my floor alone watching TV. I was particularly frightened this night for some reason, and all of a sudden, there was kicking and screaming at my door. It was like a cat screaming. It was the worst sound and really hard to describe, but it didn't sound human. I can't tell you the terror. I tried to call my boyfriend at work, but he was not reachable. So, I quickly called the local police who knew me well because I worked for the city administrator, and they were there in a flash. I told them that a woman or something was kicking and screaming at my door and then fled down the hall screeching like a cat. They searched the entire building, but found no one. I just didn't know what to make of it. Of course, I was still terrified, so I tried to call my boyfriend again, but he couldn't be reached. I told the policeman who answered the phone about what happened. Thankfully, he talked to me for quite some time, which really helped, and he said I could call him back at any time during the night if I couldn't sleep. I think it took a couple of hours, but I was so exhausted from fear that I finally fell asleep. I believe now that what I heard was otherworldly, and it was just the beginning of the terror to come.

What I am about to tell you makes me sick, and I only tell you because I want to expose the Darkness that I feel came to me through the abortions and my turning my back on God. One night, I decided to sleep on my couch in the living room, because I was still frightened by what had happened, and all of a sudden, I felt that I wasn't alone. A very heavy presence came upon me, and it was holding my arms down. I could feel it breathing on my face. I couldn't move at all. I didn't understand what was happening to me. I couldn't scream.

All of a sudden, I felt something like a claw running over me. I knew it was of a sexual nature, and I tried to fight. The presence was so strong that it was impossible to move. I felt like it was trying to rape me. Words cannot tell you of the terror. I fought and fought, and finally, it let me go. I don't remember if I prayed, but I suspect that I probably did. I didn't understand any of this at all. I had never in my life heard of things like this. I knew something of the devil and of demons, but I knew I was being physically attacked by something that was purely evil, so I couldn't really figure out what was happening to me. I couldn't imagine that they were capable of this kind of stuff. I began to hate that apartment. I cannot really recall how often this happened. I know that I never had any warning. All of a sudden, I would feel this presence on me, and I was totally helpless. I fought as hard as I could, but I didn't tell anyone because I was too afraid that I wouldn't be believed. After the first attack, sometimes, I would awake in the middle of the night and smell fire. I would jump and run into the kitchen thinking I forgot to turn off the stove, but of course, there was nothing. The smell was so intense. It was just truly awful.

One night, I was just so exhausted, and I fell into a deep sleep (on the couch, of course, because I no longer slept in my bedroom at all, unless someone was there with me). I had this dream that a figure in a long white robe and long hair was there but with his back to me. I immediately thought it was Jesus, and I was so excited. I ran to him, as a child would to his father. As the figure turned around, I knew it wasn't Jesus. His face was very beautiful, but all of a sudden, his eyes turned glowing red, and pure hatred emanated from them. I knew who it was. Suddenly, he grabbed me around the throat and started choking me. I couldn't breathe, but somewhere, in my spirit, I started yelling for Jesus. All of a sudden, I saw whom I knew to be Jesus coming into the room from my side view. I can still see His face, and it was like pure love and calm walked into the room. Just at the brief sight of Him, the devil let go of my throat and vanished. I felt the terror that the devil felt if only for an instant. When I awoke the next morning, my neck was so sore. There were no marks as I recall, but my neck was sore for quite a while. I truly believe that I had looked into the face of Satan himself and that he wanted me dead. The Bible says, "He comes to rob, kill, and destroy" (John 10:10). I knew what I was facing was powerful; I just didn't know what to do. Who would believe me, and more importantly, who would help me?

My boyfriend was off from work for the weekend, and he was staying overnight with me. I was so relieved. I think I was beginning to tell him about the devil bothering me. I remember one night, we were in my bedroom. I started to tell him about the devil, and all of a sudden, the lamp went crashing to the floor! He said to me, "Maybe, I should get my gun!' And then, he said, "Well, no, that won't do any good against this!" I think he was serious, but I'm not sure. As I recall, I would begin to tell him about my experiences, and then, I would start laughing. I think I was having a hard time believing it myself, so why should he? I didn't want him to think I was crazy. I knew that I wasn't, and after all, I didn't want to lose him.

Betsy would sometimes come to visit me. She was very distraught because she had decided to give custody of her children to their father. They were divorced. We were both devastated. I truly loved her children, and as I stated before, that was extremely unusual for me. She thought they would be better off with their father because he had a stable home. We were so sad. I was just heartbroken for her because I really understood how she felt. So, one night, she had decided to spend the night because she didn't want to be alone and neither did I. So, we were in my bedroom talking, and she said to me, "Mary, I don't think we are alone." I said, "I know," and at the end of the bed were two dark hooded figures dressed in black. We could hear them talking, but we couldn't decipher what they were saying. She and I were both terrified. We just laid there too afraid to move, and they finally left. I felt so bad that she had experienced that. I was used to it, but she wasn't, and I felt guilty about it. After all, I knew it was I whom they were after.

My sister was dating a guy who was a longshoreman. He was very nice, kind of tough, but not the kind to be afraid of things. One weekend, I was going away, and Betsy asked if she and her boyfriend could stay at my apartment. I said sure, but it didn't occur to me that the Darkness would attack them. Things were getting so bad. My sister's boyfriend told her that "he would NEVER stay in that apartment again." He wouldn't say why, but I knew things were getting really serious. My sister said he just wanted to get out of there. They packed the next morning and were "out of there" as fast as possible. I tried to get him to tell me what happened, but he wouldn't. He just said he would never go back!

Sadly, for me, my boyfriend had accepted a position in another state, and he left soon afterward. I was very devastated and cried for about two days. I wasn't much of a crier. I felt what's the use, but I couldn't help myself. I was ultimately happy for him, and I knew that I couldn't ever really be serious about anyone, and I wasn't even sure if he was serious about me. I knew that I was in trouble, though, and that I was coming apart so I was glad for him that his life went on without me. I was actually becoming afraid of him being around me, especially in his line of work. He was often in very dangerous situations, and I was afraid the devil would use that to hurt him somehow.

Not soon after he left, I had another significant dream. I was standing in front of a Blessed Mother statue. I think I was praying, but I'm not sure. The statue came to life and so very kindly said to me, "Mary, come back before it's too late." When I awoke, I was determined to do something. I had to find my way back to Jesus. I took the warning very seriously. This was the beginning of my long, arduous journey back to my faith and my freedom, and it was tough, to say the least.

CHAPTER TEN

Journey Back

He is a forgiving God who does not want his
people to perish in sin.

—2 Peter 3:9

As I said, after that dream, I knew I had to do something. I didn't
feel like I could ask the Catholic Church for help because I didn't
think they would believe me, so I somehow found a Baptist pastor.
He made an appointment to meet with me. His wife joined us, and
they were so kind, and they were very concerned about me. They
believed my story and asked me if I would consider going through a
prayer of deliverance. I agreed, although I wasn't familiar with it, but
I was willing to do anything. So, they had me sit in a chair, and they
began to pray over me for quite some time. I remember that they
asked me if I would renounce Satan and all of his works. Of course, I
said yes, and at the end of their prayer, for some inexplicable reason,
I began to foam at the mouth. It wasn't profuse, but nevertheless, it
truly happened. The couple seemed very concerned about this. I'm
not sure why, but I remember that they said to me that if I were to
die today, I would go to hell. I knew they were right, and I didn't
think they were being malicious in any way. I was very grateful to
them for their care and concern. But most of all, I was grateful that
they believed me. What a relief! I honestly cannot remember if I went

back to them or not. I liked them and knew they were deeply devout people, but I think I just went on partying and trying to forget.

Sadly, in 1981, my beloved grandfather died. I just couldn't take it and frankly still can't. One Friday evening, my sister and I decided to take Granny out to his favorite restaurant. Granny just loved it, and the food was delicious. He was eighty-nine years old at that time and still lived alone. We had a great evening together, but all of a sudden, he said, "Daughtas, I went away from here last night." Betsy and I said, "Granny, what do you mean? Where did you go and with whom?" He said that he went to a place where the singing was so beautiful and his legs didn't hurt anymore. He said, "It was balmy and the weather was beautiful." We were so shocked as the word "balmy" was not a word we thought he would ever use. He said that he didn't want to come back. He was so happy where he was but asked if he could come back to take care of some business. He said he came back to "hide a little bankbook," which he had started for Betsy and me. It had $600.00 in it, and he didn't want anyone in the family to know about it. He told us exactly where he had put it. We said, "Granny, you just can't leave us. We are so happy you came back. Please don't leave us." We had to leave it there as we just "couldn't take the thought of losing him." Well, two days later, he came out on the porch and died all alone. He had tried so hard to call all of us, but there were no cell phones then, and none of us were home. My sister and I were at a ball game in Baltimore. My parents were out shopping. My mother said a feeling came over her that she just had to get home, so she and Sully left the store and went straight home. Just as they got in the door, Granny's neighbor, Mr. Tom, an African American lovely gentleman, called to tell them that Granny was "gone." Mr. Tom was the dearest, kindest man, and he and Granny became great friends. He was so devastated, as were my parents. We all suffered so terribly knowing that my grandfather died alone. I still suffer from that guilt to this day, but I know Granny had a magnificent glimpse of heaven. It was an incredibly beautiful story that he shared with Betsy and me, and I think it was God's mercy on us to hear it as you will see.

Granny and I were sitting on the porch a couple of weeks before he died just talking. He grabbed my hands and said in his beautiful Irish brogue, "Daughta, when I die, your nerves will go, but you WILL be all right in the end." Somehow, he knew. He was so deeply spiritual. He kept rubbing my hands, and I just couldn't accept that one day, he would die. When my uncle called to tell me he was gone, I lost my mind and tried to throw myself out of the window. I don't remember this at all, but my boyfriend whom I was with at the time said he had to "tackle me." I was so grateful to have such a kind and wonderful guy in my life at that time because I couldn't take it! I just wanted to go with Granny. I was completely suicidal. I subsequently went to the funeral director who buried him and asked his thoughts about suicide. I told him I couldn't bear the world without my "Granny," not to mention my battle with the Dark. The funeral director was so kind. Thank God, he didn't call the police. He took the time to listen to me. He told me that when he picked my grandfather up after he had passed, his face was so peaceful and serene. The director went on to say that when he retrieved the bodies of people who had committed suicide, there was a look of absolute terror on their faces. He warned me not to even think about it. I thanked him for taking the time to talk to me, and in my heart, I thought that I didn't really have the courage to do it. Because, after all, I had looked into the face of the devil and his cohorts, and I didn't want to spend my eternity with them. I am telling you this, because my grandfather said the rosary for me every day. I believe his prayers saved me, but I miss him to this very day, and it's been over thirty-five years. As I said before, he gave me the greatest gift of all, which was my faith in Jesus. Sadly, my grandfather's prediction was correct. I eventually became more of a wreck than I already was, if that was even possible.

I began to feel that if I did something to help other people, maybe, the emptiness would ease up. I loved my job with the city administrator, and I didn't want to leave my boss and friends, but I was drowning. So, I decided to become a nurse. I obtained a scholarship to a nursing school at a hospital in Baltimore. I couldn't take the apartment anymore, so I decided to move back in with my parents. Soon after, my sister and I decided to get an apartment together. As

I said before, my sister had given custody of her children to their father, and we were both devastated about it. I adored her children, and I cried for about three days straight, which was very unusual for me because as I said earlier, I became very cold after the second abortion. Well, school turned out to be a disaster for me. I was so nervous. I lost about thirty pounds, and my nursing instructor, who had to be one of the coldest people in the world, told me I would never make it because I didn't have confidence in myself. Of course, I knew that it was true, but I was trying to overcome myself, but I just couldn't. So, I left nursing after I finished all of my college courses and tried to go back to secretarial work, but I couldn't. I eventually became so sick that I developed agoraphobia and panic attacks, and I began to literally live on a little love seat that my sister and I had in our apartment. If I tried to get off the couch, my head would spin and spin. It was dreadful. I think my sister thought I was just lazy. She was at her wits' end about me, and in retrospect, I feel very sorry for putting my beloved sister through so much. She eventually took me to a psychiatrist. The psychiatrist put me in the hospital and found an excellent therapist for me. I believe it took a couple of years, but with his help, I slowly was becoming strong enough to venture outside. At first, I would just walk around the apartment. Eventually, I was able to go to the bar and hang out with friends. My behavior was outrageous. Of course, the Darkness was still there. I was drinking all the time. I used booze to medicate myself. I couldn't really tolerate the psychiatric medicines too well. Most of them made me feel worse. I drank and drank and did ultimately get into drugs a bit. I loved cocaine. It made me feel like I was something. What a joke! It is totally the devil's tool. Thank God, I began to realize that it was evil because of my experiences with the darkness. So, fortunately, my bout with cocaine didn't last long. My life was dark enough without adding that to the mix. I was totally reaching the end of myself.

Finally, I had enough. I had come up with a plan to commit suicide, but I thought, *I will have to get really drunk to go through with it.* So, I drove myself to the local bar where we all knew each other. I had a friend who worked there who was a clinical social worker. Well, I got so drunk I must have said something to him that "tipped" him off. He said, "Mary, let's go outside and get some air." So, he and I went outside, and there were the police waiting for me. They were very nice but handcuffed me and drove me straight to the hospital. So, there I was, handcuffed to the bed, still alive, and terribly hungover by this time, and I knew I would be staying there for a good long while. After I was released, I said, "Enough is enough." I have got to get some help of another kind. I knew all the hospitals and doctors in the world couldn't really cure me. As I am writing this, I realize now that I owe that guy my life, because I think I was truly serious about the suicide bit. I had everything I needed in the car to do it, and at that point, I don't think I cared about the Darkness. I was in too much pain. I just wanted OUT!

CHAPTER ELEVEN

The Beginning of Freedom

You are my hiding place; you will protect me
from trouble and surround me with songs of
deliverance.

—Psalm 32:7

While I was "confined" to the couch when I was suffering from agoraphobia and panic disorder, I began to watch Jim and Tammy Faye
Bakker of the PTL Network. They were very popular televangelists in
the 1980s. I loved them, and even in their failures, I believe they were
deeply spiritual people, and I believe that they helped me so much on
my journey. I know now that sadly, they took a very wrong turn, but
they began planting a seed in me. I didn't understand about having
a personal relationship with Jesus, and I wanted to find out how to
do that. Eventually, my sister moved out, and I rented a room from a
good friend of mine. She was a very true and understanding friend. I
was happy for my sister because she had gone through enough with
me. I had become such a burden to her, and I was desperately sorry
for that. I was just so very sick by that time. As I said before, after
a long bout with therapy by a wonderful psychologist, I was able to
leave the house and eventually tried to go back "out there." Of course,
I was drunk most of the time and partying as much as I could. I was
so terribly unhappy. I tried to get back to work, and eventually, I was

able to, but I didn't do very well really. I was hungover most of the time, and my anxiety was so bad. I tried so hard to conceal it though.

Well, a couple of years went by, and I eventually rented an apartment on my own in a townhouse. It was on the second floor, and I thought I wouldn't be too afraid because my landlord was downstairs and he also had a big dog. What that would do, I don't know! I was being so attacked by the devil or demons or whatever it was. Sometimes, I felt that I was physically being held down. I could feel darkness on me. It was terrible, and I really didn't understand it at all. What I am about to tell you may be difficult to believe, but this is what happened. I was having a very hard time keeping a job because of my drinking, so I went to work for a temporary agency and waitressed in the evenings to make ends meet. One night, I came home from work around 12:00 midnight, and the phone rang. The voice on the line was kind of sickeningly sweet and taunting. It was a male's voice, and it sounded vaguely familiar. He kept saying, "You know who this is. You know who this is, don't you?"

I did answer him and said, "You sound so familiar. Who is this?" His voice began to change. and it became very gravelly and scary and very deep. He kept saying, "You know who I am," and then, he finally said, "And I want you DEAD!" I slammed the phone down and called the police. They sent someone immediately as they thought I had been followed home from work and that someone may be stalking me. They said if it happened again, they would try to trace the call. It did happen again, but only one more time, but they were unable to trace it. It was the same sickening voice, with the same sickening message. After that, I began to hear a voice that sounded exactly like my sister calling me from outside in the front yard. It was so startling, because I thought it was my sister in trouble or something. The "voice" would say, "Come outside," or just yell out my name. It almost always happened at about three o'clock in the morning. I would jump up from the couch and look out of the shades for a long time. Something always told me deep inside myself, "Don't go outside. Don't go outside!" There was never anyone there. Needless to say, it was terrifying. As I look back on it now, I wonder if it was the "Dark" trying to kill me. I don't know for sure. I have never been diagnosed as psychotic or schizophrenic and had never heard voices before. There were no more phone calls after that, but I was still experiencing the physical attacks, so I just don't know. The physical attacks were very violent really. I would be thrown or pushed sometimes. I would feel a very heavy presence on top of me "holding me down." I no longer slept in my bedroom. I was too afraid, so I slept on the couch in case I needed to escape if possible or scream downstairs to my landlord. I never told him what was happening to me though. Sometimes, the dog would bark for no reason. It was a very vicious bark and was very disturbing. My landlord would go through the house to check to see if there were any intruders, but no, there was nothing there, at least nothing you could see.

Eventually, I found myself at the Catholic Church where I went to grade school. I decided to go to Confession. Apparently, during my Confession, as the priest told me later, something I said really frightened him. He stopped in the middle of Confession and said to me, "I want you to come to the rectory first thing in the morning. Please make sure you do. I said, "Why, Father? What is wrong?" Father told me that we would talk about it in the morning and that it was very important, and then, we continued Confession. So, I did show up at 9:00 a.m. The priest had been a former Navy chaplain and was not the type to frighten easily. Father explained to me that he was a reborn, Spirit-filled Catholic priest, and I understood what he meant from watching Jim and Tammy Bakker. He and I talked and talked. I told him about everything, even the abortions. That was the first time since meeting with the Baptist couple that I let myself even think about them. He asked me if I would be willing to go through an exorcism. That "knocked me for a loop" because all I could think about was the movie that had come out in 1973. That movie was terrifying to so many people, including myself. I wouldn't even go to see it. But I said yes, and I met him at a prominent Catholic college that next week. This college was in Baltimore City and was very respected in the Catholic community. I was amazed that they permitted this. Father performed the exorcism in the chapel. He called it a minor exorcism, which meant that he didn't have to have permission from the Vatican. I honestly can't remember much about it. I didn't t know if it worked. I was still a mess when I left, but I was determined to find my way back to God, whatever it took. The priest asked me to come again for another one the following week as he didn't think I was free, which I did. I was completely overwhelmed, but I just trusted him to help me. I really don't remember much about that one either except for the candles burning, which for some reason stuck out in my mind. I forgot to mention too that I couldn't bear to be in the presence of the Eucharist or Communion at all. This was a long-time problem. I would get so nervous, and I would pace and pace in the back of the church, whatever the denomination. I was almost terrified of Communion. My heart would pound, and sometimes, I would break out in a profuse sweat and feel very nauseated. Sometimes, I would just feel like fainting.

Well, unfortunately, the priest was transferred to a parish down south, so there I was kind out there by myself. I do want to mention that he told me what had frightened him in Confession on the day that prompted him to ask me to meet him at the rectory prior to the exorcisms. He said I asked him, "Why does Jesus torment me?" Apparently, my voice changed during Confession as well. I do remember saying that though. He said this completely "shook him up!" Of course, it shook me up too! I was very sorry to see him go, and I truly appreciated his efforts to help me.

I continued to watch Tammy and Jim, and I also began to watch other televangelists. I would come home after a night of hard partying, and even in my drunkenness, I was eager to find out how to be "reborn." One day, I was invited to a wedding reception, which was to be held in a large hall, and I had stopped at the local bar first, so I was a little "tipsy" when I set off to find this reception. I pulled into the parking lot of a large hall, but I wasn't sure if it was the place. When I opened the door to the hall, I saw people praying and singing. It was kind of late, but I was drawn to go inside. I sort of forgotten about the wedding reception and wanted to see what was going on there. People came up to me and invited me to stay, which surprisingly I did. I still wanted to have another drink though. Well, this night turned out to be the turning point of my life. I cannot really remember the details, but I told people a little about myself.

They could probably tell that I had been drinking, but there I was sitting in a chair with these wonderful Christians around me praying for me. It turned out to be a nondenominational Christian fellowship called Living Water, which I began to regularly attend. I met so many wonderful people there. I began to tell them about my experiences with the Darkness. I was still experiencing it but more inwardly than the actual physical attacks that I had previously experienced.

Deep inside, I knew that there was something wrong with me. Of course, I was emotionally ill and seeing a psychiatrist and therapist still, but it was deeper than that. I eventually told the members of Living Water about the exorcisms that I had gone through, but I still was in the dark. Only Jesus knows what or who had a hold of me, but I wasn't free. Sometimes, I felt scared to look into the mirror as I was afraid I would see someone else in there besides myself. It is kind of hard to explain. Of course, I always heard a voice inside saying, "You have to die; you are nothing. You are NOTHING! JUST DIE."

I know that these very loving, Spirit-filled Christians prayed so much for me. I went through many sessions for deliverance. Sometimes, during these sessions, my limbs would contract and contort. It was very scary, but I was always able to say the name of Jesus, which I think was a good thing. I confessed all of my sins and addictions that I could think of before they set about to ask for deliverance, but I'm pretty sure I held onto the abortions. It took quite a while for me to trust anyone with that. When I told the priest about it in Confession, which I mentioned previously, I knew he couldn't tell anyone, which was an important part of Catholic Confession. Priests could not share what was heard in Confession. It was part of the canon law of the Catholic Church, so I felt safe. But this was different. I would see these people, and I was so afraid of rejection.

A wonderful couple named Dave and Allison held a weekly Bible study called "Alpha." It was started in England by a lawyer who left everything behind to become a minister. We would have a meal together, then watch a video of this minister preaching, and then pray. I loved it! I would help prepare the weekly meal, and I began to feel as if I was part of something. My intense loneliness was easing up. I had also made a good friend named Ginny. She is very dear to me, and we are still friends to this day after thirty years. I met other wonderful friends too, and I trusted them, but not with the abortions, not yet. I was still partying and drinking, though. I was also involved with a guy who as I know now could care less about me. It amazes me how deep God's love and mercy go. He didn't give up on me for a minute!

I would like to tell you something really wonderful that happened to me for a change. As I mentioned earlier, I was completely agoraphobic and was still really struggling with that, but a friend of mine had invited me to go to the beach with her and her family. For some reason, I wrongly thought I was well enough to go. We went to Virginia Beach, Virginia. This is just outside of Norfolk, Virginia, so unfortunately, all my childhood traumas came flooding back to me. When I lived in Norfolk, Aunt Jane used to take us, children, there all the time. We just loved it and had a blast! She was so wonderful, but as you know, that is where my sister and I had to go when my parents had given us up. I had become so sick that I decided to leave the condo where I was staying with my friend's family, and I got a hotel room because I couldn't bear to be with anyone at all. I tried to explain to the family, and I think the mother understood, somewhat anyway. Thank God, it was only for a weekend. I just wanted to die. I had continual panic attacks. One evening, I decided to leave my room and try walking on the beach alone to see if I could recover myself and stop the awful flashbacks. I began to pray very hard for help. As I was walking, a cloudlike thing enveloped me, and I heard a voice saying inside of me, "You are not nothing[sic]. Remember, you are not Nothing," and it so penetrated my being that I don't think I came back exactly the same. The very first thing I did when I got home was to give up a guy who I had liked for so long, but I knew he was just using me. I always knew that, but I just "hung in there" hoping for more. I remember he wanted to continue our "relationship," but I never went back. I knew I deserved so much better than that. I remember I was very sad about it though. I thought so much of him. I just wasn't willing to be treated like "NOTHING" anymore! I thank the Lord so much! I truly believe it was the Lord himself who told me that "I was NOT Nothing." Those were His exact words (even though

I know in English, it is incorrect). As you know, the devil's exact words were "You are NOTHING! You are NOTHING!" What I heard on the beach was the exact contradiction. It was an amazing experience. I believe it was the beginning of my freedom really.

I thought so much about the abortions. Jesus says, "Before I formed you in the womb, I knew you" (Jeremiah 1:5). I was thinking about the babies I destroyed. Abortion is evil, and it wreaked hell in my life, literally. My childhood was very difficult as you know and all that, but I truly believe that abortion was the thing that almost destroyed me. As you know, I also gave a child up for adoption. That was no picnic at all. Believe me when I tell you this. But nothing caused more guilt, shame, and regret than the killing of these two innocent babies. I know I'm not the only woman (or man) out there who is suffering because of abortion. My heart breaks for anyone who has had one or been party to one. But there is help through the Lord Jesus Christ. Jesus promises us that!

I became good friends with a couple at the fellowship who were devoutly Christian. The husband had a radio show, and he had invited me to be on to speak about abortion, anonymously, of course. And I did. He was not the interviewer, though. It was a woman, and I felt that she was blaming the "system" for a woman's decision to have an abortion. I took offense to that because it is a personal decision in my opinion, and one has to take responsibility for that decision and confess it to God for what it is—MURDER! She said I was being "too hard on myself," but I know that I was heading straight to Hell, literally, and that I was living with the Dark because of this. From my point of view, pro-choice is the devil's choice. I turned my back on God, the Church, my upbringing by my beloved grandfather, and everything I knew to be right and true.

CHAPTER TWELVE

The Final Exorcism

In My name shall they cast out devils.
—Mark 16:17

Jesus is so wonderful, and He led me to so many wonderful Christian friends, who tried to help me. I was fortunate enough to meet Ted at Living Water. He was a wonderful friend. He knew I was really in trouble. We would often have coffee together and talk about our pasts, and he would share with me his "coming to our Lord Jesus." It was so comforting. Ted had been led to a charismatic Episcopal church called Church of the Good Shepherd. He shared with me that he was going there initially for prayer but eventually began attending this church regularly.

He would sometimes still attend Living Water, and I always stood at the back of the service. It was very difficult for me to be at any service because I really suffered. When it was time for Communion, as I said, my body and mind would just go "ballistic." I couldn't stop pacing. I would feel sick and so upset. One day, while I was at a service at Living Water, Ted happened to be there and asked me to go with him to The Church of the Good Shepherd for prayer. Ted said that my response to that invitation so disturbed him that he knew I needed help and quickly. Thankfully, I did finally agree to go with him. When we arrived, Ted introduced me to Father Martin and the members of the prayer team. Father Martin is a deeply Spirit-filled, gifted priest and had the discernment to know that I was in trouble and that I needed an exorcism. I am not sure what I said or did during our conversation, but Father said, "Let's do it!" And I said, "Yes!" As it turned out, a priest named Father Ball just stopped by to say, "Hello." Father Martin asked him to stay and preside with him during my exorcism, and he agreed. Once the rite began, I don't remember anything about it, so I am going to share what has been told to me Father Martin and Ted as well. I do remember that Father Martin was wearing vestments though. I don't know why I remembered that, but I did. A woman named Jan was kneeling next to me on the Communion railing, and her husband and Ted stood behind me. Father Martin and Father Ball stood in front of me on the altar.

As I have said, I knew something was wrong with me, and I was so hoping this would work—that I would be "fixed" finally. During the course of the exorcism, Father Martin said that my face changed completely and that my voice changed to that of a man, deep and gravelly. Father said that during the exorcism, I said to him that "I was seeing the bear coming toward me." Can you imagine! This must have been the bear that had attacked me as a child and tormented me for so many years after. Father said that many demons spoke to him and taunted him and that, sometimes, he could talk directly to me, but most of the time, the demons would "show themselves." He said that he laughed and that made some of the demons really angry. Father Martin also said that he felt that he was finally encountering what exorcists call the "Prince" of the demons who was inhabiting me. He commanded the spirit to identify himself, and he blurted out that he was the "Spirit of Death." Father commanded it to leave me in the name of Jesus, and with that, a black form came out of me and flew up into the rafters of the church. All of a sudden, Jan, who was next to me on the Communion railing, was "attacked" by it and knocked so hard to the ground. She hit her head on the Communion railing, but thankfully was not knocked unconscious. Father said that they gathered around Jan to pray for her, she turned a shade of green, and the demon who attacked departed from her. I was becoming aware of my surroundings by then and saw this happening. Her head banged so hard on the Communion railing. I was sure that she must have been really hurt. I felt so bad about it. I knew she had taken the "hit" for me. I was told by Ted that they took Jan to the doctors after all this was over and that she was fine, no evidence of a concussion or head trauma. Thanks be to our Lord Jesus! I remember that I kept telling her how sorry I was. I was devastated. I know this is an incredible story, but it truly happened. I couldn't believe it when Father Martin told me about the "bear." I could never understand my experience with it as a child, but I knew that it was not a figment of my imagination, even though I was only six. I always wanted to die and felt that it would be better for everyone if I were dead. I was just a desperately unhappy and lonely child, and it carried on to my adulthood. I was in a terrible "battle" for most of my life!

Ted shared with me that Father Ball was not scheduled to be at the church that morning, but he felt that it was a gift from our Lord because Father Ball had assisted with many exorcisms. Father Martin had shared this with Ted and was very glad that Father Ball was able to be there. I don't know how long the actual rite took, but it was such a powerful experience. It seemed as though I came out of a bad dream. I remember that I did feel lighter afterward. I was so very grateful to our Lord Jesus Christ! I was finally free! I was, of course, so grateful to Father Martin, Father Ball, Ted, and Jan and her husband for going through such a trying experience for ME. I knew it was our Lord who set me free through the powerful prayers of these dear Christian clergy and Church members. I felt so bad that they had to go through all this "stuff." I just didn't feel that I was worth all the trouble! It took quite a long time for me to get passed that feeling, and I am still working on it.

Ted also shared with me that after I left the church that day, Father Martin, Father Ball, and Ted went through every nook and cranny of the church to make sure the demon was gone. I asked him if they had encountered any evil while doing this, and he said, "No, the Lord didn't permit it to stay." I totally agree with that, especially being in a Spirit-filled church, with such Godly, Spirit-filled Christians. They didn't want anyone who visited the Church or attended the Church regularly to be "attacked" by this spirit! I can't imagine how it must have felt to actually see this thing come out of me. Ted also told me that he promised our Lord that he would mentor me for six months. Well, that six months turned into thirty-six years! I am so grateful for all his prayers and counseling after all these years. I am sure it wasn't an easy task for him at all! I was still a "mess," but I was free of the "Dark." The unimaginable power of our Lord Jesus Christ was witnessed that day. Praise be to the Lord! His mercy endures forever!

CHAPTER THIRTEEN

A Reunion

God restores the years the locusts have eaten
away.

—Joel 2:35

I found my son in 1999 who, as I mentioned earlier, I had given up for adoption at birth. Catholic Charities handled the adoption, and when he turned twenty-one, I was allowed to have the records opened, and they hired a detective for me. I can't tell you the feelings that went through me when I got the call that they had found him. When my son called me, the first thing he said to me after I told him that I loved him was, "Thank you for not having an abortion." I went on to tell him that he was the only good thing I have ever done in my life. While I was at St. Anne's (a maternity home for unwed mothers as they used to call it), I went to Mass every day as I previously mentioned. I asked the Blessed Mother to please be his mother for me. I just knew that she would. I made him a beautiful statue of her, which I gave to him when we met. He told me that he had a "storybook life." I was so happy because I worried about him constantly. I just drank a lot to not think about it. We made arrangements for him to come to the apartment where my mother and I lived. I was so nervous that day. My sister came as did my niece, Amy, to meet him as well. I did get in touch with his father, but he said if he decided to meet with him, he would do it alone. My son's father said to me that he thought I would have been a great mother. I was shocked that he said that to me as he was just awful to me about this whole situation. At the end of our conversation, he said to me, "I never understood why you got so dark." Well, if he is reading this, I hope he gets it now! To continue, my son was awesome. He was tall and handsome. He was attending a military academy and was third in his class. He told me that he wanted to be a soldier from the time he was little. He would play "soldier" all the time. I just knew that would happen. I told him that, and I gave him some of the military records from my father and my stepfather. These records showed their awesome service to our country. He said he would put them up in his room. I was so proud of that. I was so proud of him! His parents were wonderful Christian Catholic people, and he had two adopted sisters. They were a very close family. He told me he was very close to his father. His life was every wonderful thing I had hoped it would be, and I loved the fact that he was a good Christian person. He had a good heart. God bless him, and God bless his family. I only saw him once, and I am so grateful to him for coming to see me. He didn't have to do that. I hope that he truly understood that I wanted the very best for him. Catholic Charities warned me not to expect that he would stay in touch with me. I understood that, even though it was so hard to let go of him a second time. When he drove away, I knew it would be the last time I would ever see him. His sister was driving, and he just put his hand on the car window, and I put my hand on his, and we stared at each other for quite a while before I watched them drive away. It was just too heartbreaking to describe, but I had a strange kind of peace as if I truly knew that he was okay and that I had done the very best thing for him.

A couple of years later, I met a man whom I thought that perhaps, I would marry. He had children, and I thought that now, I would be able to love children again. The relationship didn't work out, but he and I remained friends for over thirteen years. His children are like my very own. I love them so much. I have a "stepson," Noah, who is twenty. I also have my "stepchildren" named Matthew and Madison. They are the light of my life! They are twins who just turned sixteen at this time of writing. I am so very proud of them. They are so adorable and so intelligent and fun! My life truly revolves around the twins. I just want to be with them all the time! My Noah is on his own and is doing very well. He has grown up so fast! I always told Noah that I would love him for the rest of his life. It amazes me that Jesus did this for me. Jesus truly does "restore the years the locusts have eaten away" (Joel 2:25). I could never see myself loving children so much. I am grateful every day for them. My life is very full! Not that it isn't without heartache, but we all have that in one way or another. The heartaches that I experience now are totally different than the torment. I know for sure that I am delivered from the evil one. "Jesus's praise will always be on my lips" (Psalm 34:1).

My sister's children, Sean and Amy, who are now in their forties, both have children too. I love them very much. Cassidy, Amy's daughter, is nineteen, and Patrick is twenty-three. Sean, my nephew, and his wife, Karen, have two children, Megan and Melissa. They are sixteen and thirteen, respectively. When I see them, I just "light up." It's such a wonderful feeling! I have missed so much because of my insane life! It never ceases to amaze me how far God has brought me. I was so "dead!" I could never have felt this way if the Lord hadn't delivered me. I would still be sitting on a barstool somewhere, drunk as a skunk and heartbroken and at death's door if it had not been for our Lord Jesus and Father Martin, Ted, and all the wonderful Christians who helped me.

We almost lost my niece Amy because she developed MRSA in her lung. She was only thirty-two at the time. It was heart-wrenching, but through prayer and the tenacity of St. Agnes Hospital in Baltimore, she survived. She did lose her lung, but she has been able to go on fairly well. She is truly a miracle! Even the hospital calls her the "miracle girl." My poor sister, Betsy, was so devastated as we all were. I was so heartbroken for her too. I remember the day that we stopped in a Catholic Church where St. John Newman had been a priest in the 1800s. Many miracles are attributed through his intercession to the Lord. My sister let little Cassidy, who was only about seven at the time, light about thirty candles to him. Amy's husband had his minister come to pray, and the Catholic priest gave the last rites, and everyone was "hitting their knees." My dear friend and mentor Ted was praying constantly for her. I truly believe Ted has the spiritual gift of healing. My mother and I would sit in Amy's hospital room and look at her for hours. She was on a breathing machine. We just couldn't say goodbye to her. There was a peace in that room, however, which was indescribable. I believe that the Spirit of God was there and the angels too. The doctors would not give up. Thank God! How awesome is the power of prayer! We just couldn't imagine life without her!

I am very grateful to my sister, Betsy, too. I could not have endured my life without her and her children. At the time that I was going through so much torment, Sean and Amy were the only children for whom I allowed myself to feel anything. I loved them so much! I will always thank God for Betsy and her children. The Lord has given me so much!

CHAPTER FOURTEEN

A Grateful Heart

His mercy will endure forever.
—Psalm 118:29

I know that today, I am free. Who can understand the depths of the mercy of the Lord? I am no longer tormented by the Darkness. I do not hear the voice any longer who says I am nothing. I no longer hear the voice that says, "I want you dead." I am not afraid to look into the mirror anymore. I am not afraid to be in the presence of the Eucharist anymore. I can sit in church for hours without having to pace. Thanks be to the Lord!

I know this story is a dark one, but Jesus is "the light of the world" (John 8:12). He has delivered me and lifted me out of the mud. I know that if he had not done so, I would not be here today. I want you to know that I do not mean to say that I have a perfect life. After my deliverance, I still struggled with alcohol, and I developed a gambling addiction. Gambling addiction was the worse. Through the grace of God, though, the Lord has delivered me and keeps delivering me. When I was younger, I couldn't imagine life without alcohol. It took a long time to be free from that stronghold. Believe me, I am still a work in progress.

As I mentioned earlier, I have a serious panic disorder too. One day, while in prayer, I asked the Lord why He doesn't deliver me from it. In my heart, I heard Him say just like this, "Because your panic keeps you very close to me." Knowing myself, I'm sure that is true. When I was young, before my Granny died, I was very conceited and prideful. I thought I could handle anything or do anything. I am completely dependent on the Lord now. With my panic disorder comes agoraphobia, too as I shared earlier. I can only go about thirty miles from home comfortably. If I try to go any farther, my head starts to "swim." My cousin Kevin very kindly said to me one day, "You do the best that you can in the limited area in which you live." I can't tell you how much that meant to me, as he is very successful and high-powered, but he didn't judge me. I am so proud of all of my cousins, and they mean a great deal to me. They were more like brothers and sisters, as I mentioned earlier. You may remember that I lived with them as a child for four years. Sadly, because of the agoraphobia, I wasn't able to attend my aunt and uncle's funeral because they live out west. As you can imagine, it was impossible for me to even think of traveling that far, let alone fly. I just figured that when I die and am with the Lord, I will be able to go anywhere. I just try to adjust myself to it and live as productive a life as I can. You may say to yourself that I am not free. Please believe me that I am. I just truly want my life to be "about the Lord" in my own little way. I owe Him so much. His love is unfathomable.

Betsy and her children and I just loved our stepfather, Sully, as I said. Sadly, he died in 1995, and two weeks after that, my beloved Uncle Jimmy died. It was just too sad for words. Sully had a beautiful military funeral. I was so proud of him and his service to our country.

He also shared with me about two weeks before he died that he would awaken with the smell of the death camps in his nostrils. He said it was just sickening, but he just couldn't stop reliving it. It was devastating to him. I know that even though he was a "fighter" and a very seasoned soldier, he never forgot the death camps. As we know, he survived seven major battles including the Normandy Invasion, the Battle of the Bulge, and five other major campaigns. His service to this country was incredible. He was an amazing soldier, but I know he couldn't take the memory of the death camps. It haunted him until his death. What he saw with his own eyes was just UNIMAGINABLE! The unbelievable suffering he witnessed—the ovens that were packed with the bodies of the Jewish people—the starving people who were actually walking skeletons. Sully told me that he almost couldn't take it even after all he had been through in combat! The SS guards were shot on the spot. They had orders not to take them as prisoners. They made the German people in the towns near the camps march through them so they could witness the suffering and death that they had tolerated. As Sully described it, he felt that he had "seen Hell itself." He suffered from severe anxiety, and I begged him to ask the Veterans Administration to help him, but he wouldn't. I tried so hard to help him because I knew anxiety all too well. It was so overwhelmingly sad. Mom and I were together when Sully had the stroke that ultimately killed him. We were sitting in the living room, and he seemed to have such a great sense of peace about him. He actually talked about heaven, and he told me that a little bird sang to him the day before and it was so beautiful. I know he is in heaven. He shared a beautiful story with me. During the Battle of the Bulge, he said he just didn't care if he lived or died anymore and, "It was so miserable and so cold." He told me that he always wore the Blessed Mother medal that his priest had given him while he was attending Catholic school as a child. The 88s were just roaring by his head. He said he was just so fed up that he stood under a tree and held his medal and promised the Blessed Mother that he would return to the faith if he survived the war. Well, he survived all of that combat without a scratch, but he didn't keep his promise to Our Lady. He told me about it. I think this was about ten years before he died. He said that he would ask for forgiveness and go back to church. He never missed Mass after that. He and my mother went every Sunday. It was beautiful. He wore that medal until the day he died. He died with the peace of God surrounding him. I will never forget him, ever!

My dearest Uncle Jimmy suffered terribly. He lost both legs due to atherosclerosis. Uncle Lou took such good care of him, and Mom and Sully visited him every other day. He was deeply spiritual and had turned his heart back to the Lord. A Catholic priest came every week to give him Communion. He had such a spirit of peace finally.

I loved him so much, and I would go every Saturday and sit with him and talk about politics or our Lord or watch a movie together. One day, before he died, he said, "Mert, I just want to tell you that I am sorry for taking you to the racetrack. Maybe, I shouldn't have done that. You were much too little!" I said, "Uncle Jimmy, it was my favorite thing to do. We had such a good time together. I just loved to be with you." And I truly meant that! I loved him so much! I was so sad at his funeral that I couldn't even cry. It took me a couple of years to do so. I was in so much pain.

I was crushed that I couldn't go to my Aunt Jane's funeral (nor Uncle Gene's either) because of my severe agoraphobia. Something very beautiful happened though. I always told my aunt about my panic disorder, but unless you have it yourself, it is very hard to understand. Well, shortly after her death, I had a very vivid dream in which she came to me. She was completely herself, personality, looks, etc., but her face was translucent, and she was shining. She said to me, "Mary, I didn't understand why you didn't come to see me, but I understand everything now."

I said to her, "Aunt Jane, how am I going to take this? How am I going to say goodbye?"

She just smiled at me and said, "Don't worry. It will all be okay." I woke up feeling such a peace, because it was haunting me that I couldn't be with her. I really wanted to try to go out west to see her before she died, but my doctor strongly cautioned me against it. In my heart, I know he was right, but I really loved her, and I was so worried that she wouldn't know it. I think this was just another one of the Lord's mercies to me. I had the feeling that she completely understood.

My little Aunt Julie whom I loved so much died at age sixty-one. It was so devastating. She had suffered such a long time with lupus and ultimately died of a stroke. She is survived by her husband, Bob, and her two boys. Bob and I have stayed very close through all these losses. It has been "tough going" as my Sully used to say. My uncle PeeWee is my dad's only surviving sibling. He is a very wonderful person too! I do hope to be able to see him soon.

Sadly, as of this writing, my beloved Betsy died from lung cancer. I can't tell you how much I miss her, but I know she had the incredible faith that Granny had passed on to us. I know that she is in heaven with our Lord. I am just so brokenhearted at losing her though! One day, she and I were sitting at my table having coffee, and she said to me, "Mary, why didn't anyone want us?" I was so sad as we hardly ever talked about these things. I looked at her and said, "Betsy, I just don't know, but I really love you, and I wouldn't have survived life without you." That was our very last conversation.

My dear Uncle Lou died two years after, and my mom died two years after my Uncle Lou. The losses have been staggering really. Six months after my Betsy passed away, my stepchildren's father died of lung cancer. He was only fifty-four. He was like a brother to me, and we fought like brothers and sisters do, but I was devastated. I am still grieving all the losses, but I know our Lord is with me. I just want to share with you that my mother had Alzheimer's disease. I took care of her for almost twenty years. The doctors told me that she survived so long with this terrible disease because of the love and care that she had received from me. I had totally forgiven my mother for all the pain and suffering that I had gone through as a child. She told me that she was truly sorry for everything, and when she was dying, she said, "Mary Ellen, I will never forget you. Jesus is here now, and I have to go." There was such a presence in that room—it was indescribable! The incredible thing was that she had lost her speech but when she was in the presence of the Lord, she spoke clearly. It was amazing to see. She had a complete look of peace at her passing. I told my cousin Ellen about it, and she spoke about it in the beautiful eulogy she had given for my mother. She and my cousin Patty were such terrific support for me during that period. I will never forget their kindness to me. I finally had felt that my mother "loved me." I just didn't want to let her go!

CHAPTER FIFTEEN

God Uses the Broken

…Though our outer self is wasting away, our inner self is being renewed day by day. For this light momentary affliction is preparing for us an eternal weight of glory beyond all comparison… for the things that are seen are transient, but the things that are unseen are eternal.

—2 Corinthians 4:16–18

After my mother had died, I moved to the Eastern Shore. I took a little part-time job at a local drug store. Everyone was very nice there, and my boss had such a kind and understanding heart. Well, as I have mentioned, I suffer from an anxiety disorder. I was beginning to have some kind of attack at work. My doctor and I thought it was the anxiety disorder "kicking in" because of all the losses that I had recently gone through. I would get very weak, and my boss would let me sit down until it passed. This just kept happening.

One day, I had gone to the grocery store and stocked up, and while returning home, I passed a young little teenage girl who was walking along a very long road near my house. It was cold that day, and when I got home, I felt worried about her. I unloaded my groceries and decided to go back to see her. Something also told me to stop at the Kent Island–Anne Arundel Medical Center to see if I could get an appointment since I was going back out. I just don't know where that came from as my doctor was in Laurel, but I felt an urgency to be seen. She was still walking when I got back to the main road, so I pulled over and asked her, "Do you need a ride home? I know this is a long walk, and I would be happy to help. I also brought you a bottle of water if you would like one." She came over to my window and was the sweetest little person.

The first thing she said to me was "Please take good care of yourself." She said, "I am fine. Don't worry about me, but thank you for asking." She came back to my window before I pulled off and said, "Please take good care of yourself," and I promised her that I would and that I was going to see about getting a doctor's appointment nearby! So, I pulled away, and as I was driving to the doctor, I decided to turn around to see her—I don't know why, but I can't explain it—but she was gone. I was so deeply touched by her concern for me. It was beautiful really. I don't think I would have gone back out at all if I hadn't been touched by her. Fortunately, I went straight to the Medical Center. This practice wasn't taking new patients, but they said if I changed to their practice, they would fit me in within the hour. I was grateful because I felt sure that I had a very bad sinus infection because of the pain and pressure. I was continually having vertigo. I was able to see a practitioner named Mackenzie, and I told her about what was happening to me at work. I asked her if she thought we should do a CT scan to see if I had a bad sinus infection. She had me go straight to the radiology department down the hall, and they took me right away. I had a CT scan and was told that my doctor should have the results in about a day or two. Well, I received a call that night at about 7:30 p.m. from Mackenzie, and she told me that, unfortunately, I had two brain tumors. She said she was so sad to call and tell me that. She informed me that she would make an appointment for me with a neurosurgeon who was excellent and would get back to me the next morning. Of course, she tried to get me in as quickly as possible. I know she saved my life! I will always remember her. I saw the neurosurgeon the very next week, and I was scheduled for surgery within a week of that visit. My neurosurgeon was a very spiritual, wonderful doctor, and he told me that my chances were "fairly" good but that I should get everything in order because "I could possibly die, especially because of my age." He said, "If you were my sister, I would absolutely tell you to have the surgery. We won't know if it is cancer until we remove the tumors." I said, "Doctor, thank you for being so honest with me." I did exactly what he had said. I was totally ready to leave this world if it was my time. I had the last rites from my priest, I made all my final arrangements, and I packed everything in my room because something told me that I wouldn't be back. I felt the Lord Jesus tell me to check out a book called *The Hiding Place*, which was a book about Corrie Ten Boom who was in the Dutch resistance during World War II. She was captured and sent to Ravensbrück, which was a notorious death camp. She suffered terribly, but she survived. She ministered to the entire world with her story. She had such a deep faith in Jesus, and it was incredible. This is totally true. I was told in the deep part of my heart to turn to page 55, which told the story of Corrie's aunt, Tante Jans. She suffered terribly from fear of death and anxiety! I couldn't believe that I was in the same shape as she was, though she was told that she had three weeks to live. Tante Jans broke down and cried and said the Lord told her, "Your hands may be empty, but all you need to do is believe in me and that I died on the Cross for you." I knew my hands were "empty" but thanks be to God, I truly believed in the power of the Cross and that Jesus had died for me. This gave me such peace and assurance that all would be okay no matter which way it turned out.

Well, my boyfriend took me to the hospital for my surgery. I thank God for him and pray for him every day! We had to be there at 5:00 a.m. I was a little sad, but I wasn't shaking or scared. The Lord had such mercy on me. I just felt so compelled to share with you the grace He gave to me to face this. My boyfriend and some of his family were there as great support. My neurosurgeon said that the operation should take about four hours, but it actually turned out to be an eight-hour surgery. What I am telling you truly happened to me. During the course of the surgery, I left my body. My soul began to soar upward and upward. The colors were just gorgeous, and I passed beautiful mountains, and I saw my sister, Betsy. We just smiled at each other. I was so happy. After that, I kept soaring upward and upward. Well, I finally stopped soaring, and Jesus, the Blessed Mother, St Joseph, and St. Peter were waiting for me. It was just amazing! St. Peter told me who he was, and I said, "I love you! I am so happy to meet you!" I knew who St. Joseph was and, of course, the Blessed Mother. Our Lady was wearing a beautiful long royal blue veil. She was standing very close to our Lord. They were just smiling at me so lovingly. I am not sure if I was outside of heaven or what. Jesus, Our Lady, St. Joseph, and St. Peter began to talk among themselves. I don't remember at all what was said, but I was brought back. They accompanied me, and when I was coming out of the anesthesia, they were in my room with me. It was just amazing! I know it sounds unbelievable, but it is true. I was brought back for a reason, but I wasn't told why. They didn't stay very long, but I can still see their faces smiling at me. I was still groggy, but I could see them with my human eyes. I still can't believe it! I lifted my hand to say goodbye! I wasn't able to talk yet. For about three to four weeks after this incredible experience, I felt as if I was between heaven and earth. It was indescribable peace! When I slept, it felt like I was sleeping on air. My soul was so light. When I saw my neurologist for a follow-up, I asked him if I had died during the surgery. He had all my records from my neurosurgeon. He said no, but he shared with me that my surgery went "very badly after about four hours." He didn't expound on it, but I told him my story about leaving my body. I am not sure if he believed me, but he did listen. Just to let you know, the whole surgical team came in a couple of days later after my surgery. They wanted to tell me that my tumors were noncancerous. This touched me so deeply as to how much they cared about me!

Well, I have prayed very hard as to why I came back. I am doing just fair physically so far, but I felt compelled to tell you my story to warn of the dangers of abortion. I am very scared for anyone who has had an abortion or has been involved with abortion. I feel that I opened the door to Satan after doing that and telling the Lord how much I rejected Him! I am very afraid for my country that we are permitting this. There is such a spirit of hatred and death that is permeating the very core of this beloved land that my father and stepfather so valiantly fought for. I know many of you out there can say the same about your own family members. I am sure we don't want this kind of hate! I love my country very much, but I think abortion is only going to bring disaster to us. I hope that anyone considering abortion won't do it, and if you have done it, please go to the Lord about it. He will help you. You can trust Him. Project Rachel is an excellent place to begin or a trusted pastor or clergyman. I pray daily for deep healing and peace on our land and the end of the scourge of hatred and violence that I believe abortion is causing. Let's all pray together no matter what faith we are! I pray that we will love each other no matter what our politics, or race, or color! We can work out our differences! I believe the "Darkness" has been let loose in our country. I truly do. If we turn to the Lord, we will be okay! In the Bible, Jesus says, "Before I formed you in the womb, I knew you, and before you were born, I set you apart..." (Jeremiah 1:5). This verse deeply touched me after my final exorcism. Jesus knows us before we are born. I know I will see my two babies in heaven when I die. I actually had a dream about it. I can't even express the mercy our Lord has had on me!

I want to expose the "Darkness." He is a powerful foe. As I mentioned previously in the book, the Bible says, "What is done in the dark will be brought to the light..." (Luke 8:17). If anyone out there is in the Dark, please get to know Jesus. He is truly the way out. There is healing, and there is hope through Him. I know this for sure. His praise will always be on my lips. As the Bible says in Psalm 32:7, "You are my hiding place; you will protect me from trouble and surround me with songs of deliverance." I can assure you that the Lord has done that for me, and he will do that for you too. It isn't just an empty promise, but it is the Truth. You can count on it!

The President of the United States takes pleasure in presenting the PRESIDENTIAL UNIT CITATION to the

SIXTH MARINE DIVISION, REINFORCED

consisting of: The Sixth Marine Division; First Marine War Dog Platoon; Fifth Provisional Rocket Detachment; Third Platoon, First Bomb Disposal Company; Marine Observation Squadron Six; Sixth Joint Assault Signal Company; First Armored Amphibian Battalion; Fourth Amphibian Tractor Battalion; Ninth Amphibian Tractor Battalion; First Section, Second Platoon, First Bomb Disposal Company; 708th Amphibian Tank Battalion, U. S. Army; Third Armored Amphibian Battalion (less 4 platoons); 91st Chemical Mortar Company (Separate), U. S. Army; First Platoon, Company B, 713th Armored Flame-Thrower Battalion, U. S. Army,

for service as set forth in the following

CITATION:

"For extraordinary heroism in action against enemy Japanese forces during the assault and capture of Okinawa, April 1 to June 21, 1945. Seizing Yontan Airfield in its initial operation, the SIXTH Marine Division, Reinforced, smashed through organized resistance to capture Ishikawa Isthmus, the town of Nago and heavily fortified Motobu Peninsula in 13 days. Later committed to the southern front, units of the Division withstood overwhelming artillery and mortar barrages, repulsed furious counterattacks and staunchly pushed over the rocky terrain to reduce almost impregnable defenses and capture Sugar Loaf Hill. Turning southeast, they took the capital city of Naha and executed surprise shore-to-shore landings on Oruku Peninsula, securing the area with its prized Naha Airfield and Harbor after nine days of fierce fighting. Reentering the lines in the south, SIXTH Division Marines sought out enemy forces entrenched in a series of rocky ridges extending to the southern tip of the island, advancing relentlessly and rendering decisive support until the last remnants of enemy opposition were exterminated and the island secured. By their valor and tenacity, the officers and men of the SIXTH Marine Division, Reinforced contributed materially to the conquest of Okinawa, and their gallantry in overcoming a fanatic enemy in the face of extraordinary danger and difficulty adds new luster to Marine Corps history, and to the traditions of the United States Naval Service."

For the President,

James Forrestal

Secretary of the Navy

Delivered to Sergeant Tommie
(n) GRAVES, (898945), USMC.
25 July, 1949.

4Jul44, emb and sailed from Advance Base Section, NavSupDep, Bayonne,
N.J., via USS SABIK; 18Jul44, arr and disemb at Espiritu Santo, New
Hebrides; 26Jul44, emb and sailed fr Espiritu Santo, New Hebrides,
via USS SABIK; 29Jul44, arr and sailed fr Guadalcanal, British
Solomon Islands; 31Jul44, arr and disemb at Pavuvu, Russell Islands.

LOUIS W. DAVIS, 1st Lt. USMCR,
Troop Commander.

HEADQUARTERS AND SERVICE COMPANY, FOURTH MARINES, 6TH MAR DIV.
14Mar   embarked aboard U.S.S. MC INTYRE at GUADALCANAL, B.S.I.
15Mar45 sailed. 16-31Mar45 enroute. 1Apr45 arrived and disembarked
at OKINAWA SHIMA, RYUKYU ISLANDS. 1Apr45-6Jul45 participated in
action against the enemy on OKINAWA SHIMA, RYUKYU ISLANDS. 7Jul45
embarked aboard U.S.S. DU PAGE AT OKINAWA SHIMA, RYUKYU ISLANDS.
8Jul45 sailed. 9-13Jul45 enroute. 14Jul45 arrived and disembarked
at GUAM, MARIANAS GROUP.

R.A. THOMPSON
1stLt, U.S.M.C.R.
Commanding.

EXPEDITIONS—ENGAGEMENTS—COMBAT RECORD

Participated In (Battle or campaign)	From—	To—(Incl.)

Remarks: (Recommendations for awards, wounds received; distinguished service, etc.)

MEDALS—DECORATIONS—COMMENDATIONS

Description—Type of Medal or Badge	Number, if any	Awarded by	Signature of Certifying Officer
Good Conduct Medal 1943-46			
Asiatic Pacific Medal w/1star			
Victory Medal World War II			
China Service Medal			
And PUC 25Jul49			Transcribed from old SRB
National Def Serv Medal		President U.S.	W.A. Burkans 1stLt
Korean Service w/**			
American Defense			
Purple Heart w/**			Transcribed fr old SRB
Good Conduct Medal (2d Awd)		CO,H&SBN,2dCSG,FMF,CLNC	Capt,MC

GRAVES	Tommie	(n)	898945
(LAST NAME)	(First)	(Middle)	(Serial No.)

NAVMC 118(9)-PD

9 ____

100

NAVJAG-471 (6-54)

DEPARTMENT OF THE NAVY
OFFICE OF THE JUDGE ADVOCATE GENERAL
WASHINGTON 25, D. C.

In The Board of Review, U. S. Navy
Before

E. J. BODZIAK, KENNETH B. HAMILTON, AND Z. W. NEFF

NCM 59 00706

U N I T E D   S T A T E S

v.

Tommie (n) GRAVES
Acting Gunnery Sergeant (E-6)
898945
U. S. Marine Corps

Review pursuant to Article 66(c), UCMJ,
of special court-martial convened by
Commanding Officer, Headquarters
Battalion, at Marine Corps Schools,
Quantico, Virginia.
Sentence adjudged 31 March 1959.

Decided   12 May 1959

LTCOL Remmel H. Dudley, USMC, Appellate Defense Counsel
LT Gailen L. Keeling, USN, Appellate Government Counsel

D E C I S I O N

Upon trial by special court-martial, the accused pleaded
guilty to violation of Article 86, one specification of un-
authorized absence of about 99 days, Uniform Code of Military
Justice. He was sentenced to be discharged from the service
with a bad conduct discharge, confinement at hard labor for
six months, forfeiture of $130.00 per month for a like period
and reduction to the grade of private. Three previous convictions
were considered. The convening authority reduced the forfeitures
to $43.00 per month for six months but otherwise approved the
findings of guilty and the sentence. Upon advice of his staff

☆ U. S. GOVERNMENT PRINTING OFFICE—1958—337508

legal officer, the supervisory authority noted that the court-
martial erroneously considered the conviction of the accused
by general court-martial (Prosecution Exhibit 2) and reassessed
the sentence by reducing the confinement and forfeitures to
five months but otherwise approving the findings of guilty and
the sentence.

Appellant assigns as error that the confinement and forfeitures
are unduly severe. To support the contention that the confinement
and forfeitures are unduly severe appellate defense counsel urges
upon us to consider the long period of previous good service, his
personal family problems, and the various awards and decorations
which the accused has earned as the result of his service through-
out the last two wars. It is further urged that since the
accused is not going back to duty that confinement in this case
will serve no purpose. With this last contention we do not agree.
With more than fifteen (15) years of active service it is to the
accused's interest to be returned to duty. The accused will
have ample opportunity at the Retraining Command to demonstrate
his fitness for further service. Considering the gravity of the
offense of which he stands convicted, his status as a senior
noncommissioned officer at the time of the commission of the
offense, and giving full weight to the mitigating and extenuating
factors which appear in the record of trial,it is our opinion

Tommie (n) GRAVES
NCM 59 00706

that the sentence as approved on review below is appropriate
and legal.

Accordingly, the findings of guilty and the sentence as
approved on review below, are affirmed.

E. J. BODZIAK

KENNETH B. HAMILTON, Concurs

Z. W. NEFF, Concurs

NAVJAG-471 (6-54)

DEPARTMENT OF THE NAVY
OFFICE OF THE JUDGE ADVOCATE GENERAL
WASHINGTON 25, D. C.

In The Board of Review, U. S. Navy
Before

E. J. BODZIAK, KENNETH B. HAMILTON, AND Z. W. NEFF

NCM 59 00706

U N I T E D   S T A T E S

v.

Tommie (n) GRAVES
Acting Gunnery Sergeant (E-6)
898945
U. S. Marine Corps

Review pursuant to Article 66(c), UCMJ,
of special court-martial convened by
Commanding Officer, Headquarters
Battalion, at Marine Corps Schools,
Quantico, Virginia.
Sentence adjudged 31 March 1959.

Decided   8 June 1959

LTCOL Remmel H. Dudley, USMC, Appellate Defense Counsel
LT Cailen L. Keeling USN, Appellate Government Counsel

D E C I S I O N
ON MOTION FOR RECONSIDERATION

This case was decided by this Board on 12 May 1959 and
now comes before us again on Motion for Reconsideration filed
by appellant. Our attention is invited to the fact that the
accused, by a previous conviction, has been sentenced to a
bad conduct discharge, and it is urged that with two punitive
discharges adjudged against him the chances of the accused
to be returned to duty are remote. It is contended that for
the foregoing reason the sentence to confinement and forfeitures
will serve no purpose and should be remitted. While possible
rehabilitation of the accused is one of the paramount

☆ U. S. GOVERNMENT PRINTING OFFICE—1955—337508

considerations in any determination of an appropriate sentence
this is not to say that the deterrent factor taken into con-
sideration is of less importance. We have reconsidered the
record together with the very persuasive brief of appellate
defense counsel and after weighing the gravity of the offense,
the position of the accused as a senior non-commissioned officer,
and his record of three previous convictions, have determined
that the sentence, as approved on review below, is appropriate
under the circumstances of this case. The motion for reconsideration is denied.

E. J. BODZIAK

KENNETH B. HAMILTON, Concurs

Z. W. NEFF, Concurs

ABOUT THE AUTHOR

Mary Graves's father was a US Marine, and she was born in Bethesda Naval Hospital in Maryland. She is very proud of his service to our country, but as you will see, so many tragedies happened to him and to her and her family. She hopes you will read her book. It is very dark, but there is tremendous healing and deliverance at the end. The light of Christ shines through the darkness. She has looked into the face of evil, and she assures you that God is stronger.

She wants to thank Father Martin and her mentor, Ted, for everything that was done for her. She does not believe that she would still be alive today if not for their intercession; in fact, she is sure of it. She would like to tell you that if you should ever want to reach her, please feel free to call Page Publishing as they will direct you. She would be truly honored to speak to anyone who may be in the dark. If nothing else, she would completely understand.